"ALCHEMY OF ACCOMPLISHMENT"

INSTRUCTIONS OF MOUNTAIN DHARMA; HEART GUIDANCE ON THE PRACTICE, EXPRESSED IN AN EASY-TO-UNDERSTAND WAY

BY DUDJOM RINPOCHE
JIGDRAL YESHE DORJE

TONY DUFF
PADMA KARPO TRANSLATION COMMITTEE

This text is secret and should not be shown to those who have not had the necessary introduction and instructions of the Thorough Cut system of Dzogchen meditation. If you have not had the necessary instructions, reading this text can be harmful to your spiritual health! Seal. Seal. Seal.

First edition, September 2008
ISBN: 978-9937-9031-3-4

Janson typeface with diacritical marks and
Tibetan Classic typeface
Designed and created by Tony Duff
Tibetan Computer Company
http://www.tibet.dk/tcc

Produced, Printed, and Published by
Padma Karpo Translation Committee
P.O. Box 4957
Kathmandu
NEPAL

Web-site and e-mail contact through:
http://www.tibet.dk/pktc
or search Padma Karpo Translation Committee on the web.

CONTENTS

INTRODUCTION

Dudjom Jigdral Yeshe Dorje, born in 1904 in Tibet, was the first incarnation of the great treasure revealer Dudjom Lingpa [1835–1904]. Dudjom Rinpoche passed away in the 1990's and two of his incarnations were recognized very shortly after.

The text presented here is a record of a discourse by Dudjom Rinpoche, Jigdral Yeshe Dorje on the retreat practice of Great Completion[1]. The discourse was given to a group of retreatants at one of his retreat centres, as mentioned in the colophon of the text, concerning the practice of "mountain dharma". Mountain dharma is the dharma practised by people who actually go and do serious practice away from civilization which was, in Tibet, usually far off in the mountains, hence the name.

The text is a particularly clear exposition of what someone who wants to spend their life practising the profound dharma

[1] Tib. rdzogs pa chen po. Dzogchen.

of Great Completion should do. It is very famous in the Dudjom lineage for being an excellent text for anyone wanting to practise Great Completion dharma and is read widely by practitioners of other lineages of Great Completion, too. One of the qualities of the text is that it was given using colloquial language in a straight-from-the-heart way, so much so that even the title includes this point. This quality can be seen clearly in the Tibetan. This does not mean that the unique and technical language of the depths of Great Completion practice have been skipped over. To the contrary, the explanations use all of the technical language as needed but couch it in a way of talking that comes from and does go straight to the heart. Hopefully, the clarity, practicality, and straight-from-and-to the heart quality of the original comes through in this English translation.

The text gives a complete set of instructions for retreat according to the Great Completion system of practice. It clearly states the foundation work that has to be done, including development of a mind for retreat. After that, it gives details of Thorough Cut practice for the main practice but does not give any instruction in the other main practice of Great Completion, Direct Crossing[2]. It ends with a series of injunctions about how to put this all together in one life so that the path really does work for a person.

I was asked about the text in 2007 by the Western Tulku Nyinje who was learning the Dudjom system of practice at

---

[2] Thorough Cut and Direct Crossing—in Tibetan, Thregcho and Thogal respectively—are the two main practices of innermost Great Completion.

the time. I had read an early translation of this text made in 1978 but when I now compared that with the Tibetan version, I found that the early translation was mistaken or misleading in many places. Therefore, I decided to re-translate the text for the Western tulku and, having done so, thought to make it available to others who could benefit from it. The result is this book.

Our Supports for Study

I have been encouraged over the years by all of my teachers and gurus to pass on some of the knowledge I have accumulated in a lifetime dedicated to the study and practice, primarily through the Tibetan Buddhist tradition, of Buddhism. On the one hand they have encouraged me to teach. On the other hand, they are concerned that, while many general books on Buddhism have been and are being published, there are few books that present the actual texts of the tradition. They and many other, closely involved people have encouraged me to make and publish high quality translations of individual texts of the tradition.

In general, we have published a wide range of books that present the important literature of Tibetan Buddhism. In particular, the author of this text is one of the key figures in the transmission of the most profound level of Great Completion teachings in Tibet and we have published many of the important texts of that system, with each one carefully selected to inform about a particular aspect of that teaching. Other titles of ours that lay out the whole system and which are important to read in conjunction with this one are *The*

Feature of the Glorious, Expert King by Patrul Rinpoche, *About the Three Lines* by Dodrupchen III, *Alchemy of Accomplishment* by Dudjom Jigdral Yeshe Dorje, *Hinting at Dzogchen* by Tony Duff, *Peak Doorways to Emancipation* by Shakya Shri, and so on. These books are all essential reading for Thorough Cut practitioners, and we are adding other, similar titles all the time.

All in all, you will find many books both for free and for sale on our web-site, all of them prepared to the highest level of quality. Many of our books are available not only on paper but as electronic editions that can be downloaded, and all of them are prepared to the highest level of quality. We encourage you to look at our web-site to see what we have; the address is on the copyright page at the front of this book. Major book sellers also carry our paper editions.

It has also been a project of ours to make tools that non-Tibetans and Tibetans alike could use for the study and translation of Tibetan texts. As part of that project, we prepare electronic editions of Tibetan texts in the Tibetan Text input office of the Padma Karpo Translation Committee and make them available to the world. Tibetan texts are often corrupt so we make a special point of carefully correcting our work before making it available through our web-site. Thus, our electronic texts are not careless productions like most Tibetan texts found on the web but are highly reliable editions that can be used by non-scholars and scholars alike. Moreover, many of the texts are free. The Tibetan text for this book is available for download as a free, electronic edition. It is also included at the back of the book as an aid to serious study.

The principal lineage teachers of innermost Great Completion as it came into Tibet including Garab Dorje, the source of the teaching in general and the Three Lines teaching in particular. Garab Dorje above left, Manjushrimitra above right, Vimalamitra below left, Shri Singha below right of Padmasambhava in the centre. Mural on the wall of Dzogchen Monastery, Tibet, 2007. Photograph by the author.

Our electronic texts can be read, searched, and so on, using our Tibetan software. The software can be used to set up a reference library of these texts and then used to read and even research them quickly and easily. The software, called TibetD and TibetDoc, has many special features that make it useful not only for reading but also for understanding and even translating texts. One key feature is that you can highlight a Tibetan term in a text then look it up immediately in any of our electronic dictionaries. We suggest the highly acclaimed *Illuminator Tibetan-English Dictionary* as the best dictionary for the purpose. As with all of our publications, the software and electronic texts can be obtained from our web-site whose address is on the copyright page at the front of the book.

Health Warning

The text here is about a subject that is usually kept very secret. Therefore, I have translated the text as is, providing footnotes where needed but have deliberately not given any further explanation or commentary of the meaning. The text is unusually clear, so that anyone who has had the oral teachings needed to understand the material will be able to understand them or at least go to a teacher and ask for an explanation. Anyone who has heard these teachings in person from a qualified teacher, and especially who has had the introduction to the nature of mind[3] around which the teachings hinge, please use the text as you will.

---

[3] Introduction to the nature of mind is mostly mis-translated these days as "pointing out" instruction.

If you have not heard these teachings and if you have not had a proper introduction to the nature of your mind, you would probably be better off not reading this book but seeking out someone who could teach it to you. These days there are both non-Tibetans and Tibetans who can do that for you and who are fairly readily available in many countries across our planet. In short, the contents of this book could be dangerous to your spiritual health if you are not ready for it, so exercise care. Let me add that I have many times in the last few years run into young men who are extremely confident of their understanding of the meaning of the profound teachings of Great Completion but who just spout words that they have read in books. The solidity of their minds is noticeable. Unfortunately, they have read the books and know the words but have not contacted the inner meaning that the books are intended to be merely a pointer towards. That is a very dangerous position to be in, a point which is echoed by Dudjom Rinpoche in this text.

Tony Duff
Swayambunath,
Kathmandu,
Nepal
August 1st, 2008

"ALCHEMY OF ACCOMPLISHMENT" INSTRUCTIONS OF MOUNTAIN DHARMA; HEART GUIDANCE ON THE PRACTICE EXPRESSED IN AN EASY-TO-UNDERSTAND WAY

THE PREFACE

I respectfully prostrate at the feet of the glorious, holy guru of unequalled kindness and take refuge in him. Grant your blessings that for I and my followers, an un-distorted realization of the profound path will quickly arise in our mind-streams so that we then seize in this very life the seat of rulership which is the primordial state.

Now in regard to that[4], here, on this occasion, which is a very pure kind of karmic fortune that is the result of previously made aspirations, I will, for those fortunate persons[5] who put their trust from their hearts in the dharma of the profound secret Great Completion and in the guru who reveals it and who wish to be escorted to the very end of practice, provide the entrance they need by them by explaining in an easy-to-

[4] This phrase is the standard Tibetan phrase used to indicate that the preliminaries of a discourse are done with and now one is going to give the discourse itself.

[5] See glossary.

understand way that puts what they need right in their hands, the instructions of the key points of mountain dharma, given as an innermost guidance on the practice of the very secret Great Completion[6], in an easy-to-understand way that puts it right in your hand[7]. The explanation is understood through its three main topics:

1. The introduction: the way to train the mind-stream in which the bindings of attachment and clinging are severed and rational mind[8] is bound over to the service of dharma;

2. The main part: the way in which the exaggerations of view, meditation, and conduct are severed[9] then accomplishment is undertaken by entering the narrow avenue of practice.

---

[6] There are several levels of Great Completion teaching. Very secret here does not mean very secret in general but refers to the innermost of Great Completion teaching.

[7] Dudjom Rinpoche was speaking to his disciples who were in three year retreat and was saying to them, "Our gathering here is a time at which the karmas planted by our various prayers of aspiration in former times have ripened and come together to make this very pure occasion on which we together could look at the very deep dharma of complete purity, meaning enlightenment, in the form of the dharma of Great Completion. To give you the means to enter its practice, I will give you an explanation of that dharma in the form of a guidance that is like my heart's blood.

[8] See glossary.

[9] See glossary.

3. The post-attainment[10]: the way to maintain samaya vows and include this life's activities within dharma.

[10] See glossary.

INTRODUCTION: TAMING THE MIND STREAM

I will talk a little about this.

My goodness! This flickering on and off of rigpa[11], our so-called "mind"[12], did originally arise simultaneous with Samantabhadra but Samantabhadra was liberated through self-knowledge whereas each of us sentient beings wandered on into endless cyclic existence through non-recognition[13]. Each of us has taken a countless number of bodies of the six classes and everything we have done has been meaningless. Now, on this occasion, when we have obtained that one in a hundred chance of a human body, if we do not do something to prevent birth in the rotten destinies of cyclic existence, there is no certainty of where we will be born after dying and, no matter which birth we take in the six classes of migrators, it

---

[11] See glossary.

[12] The word "mind" used by itself throughout this book refers to Tib. sems, the word used specifically to indicate samsaric mind.

[13] The point is that you either recognize your own rigpa or do not. If you do, you are enlightened. If not, you gain "not rigpa'-ing" usually translated as "ignorance" and that is the path of samsara.

will never be anything but unsatisfactory. We might have obtained this human body but even that is not enough; death is not fixed so right now we must start a genuine practice of dharma. More than that, at the point of death we need, just like Jetsun Mila, to have no regrets and no embarrassment over what we have done; he said,

> "I, Milarepa, have no embarrassment over
> My own practice of dharma."

We might enter the dharma path but it is not enough just to adopt the appearance of a dharma practitioner. It is necessary to cut all the activities that we set up for ourselves because of thinking of this life, all the ties to sensuality. When they have not been severed, our weak minds might engage once in dharma but, as soon as we meet our attachments to homeland, wealth and possessions, relatives, close friends, and so on, that mind of attachment becomes the cause, the object of attachment becomes the condition, and the joining of the two results in an obstacle made by mara[14]; we resume our association with ordinary worldly people then revert to the karmic extreme[15]. Thus, we must reduce our needs for food, clothes, and talk and then, remaining uninvolved with the eight worldly dharmas, one-pointedly wrap up our rational minds in dharma, doing just like Conqueror Yang Gonpa who said,

---

[14] See glossary.

[15] Extremes here means that we engage in karma as the final goal, not the opposite which was the beyond karma goal that we were following in the dharmic path.

"In an isolated place where the thought of death hits
the heart,
The practitioner who turns away clinging from
deep down
Stays in retreat with all concerns for this life let go
Never meeting people with a mind of the eight
dharmas."

Not doing that but mixing our dharma with the eight dharmas would be disastrous because it would be the same as eating food mixed with poison.

If we sum these eight dharmas up, they come down to two, namely hope and fear, and they are none other than the pair, attachment and aversion. The internal attachment and aversion pose externally as Gyalpo and Senmo[16] so, for as long as we do not separate rational mind from attachment and aversion, we will not be separated from Gyalpo and Senmo, with the result that obstacles will never end. Therefore, we must examine ourselves again and again, looking deep into mind and asking, "Are these eight dharmas, the conceited attachment to this life, present in me?", then, if they are, we must assiduously rid ourselves of these faults. Harbouring the eight dharmas in mind while outwardly showing the appearances of a true dharma follower and obtaining articles through such deceit is another type of wrong livelihood[17].

---

[16] Gyalpo is a neuter demon that personifies the root affliction of ignorance in its various forms and Senmo is a female demon that personifies the root affliction of desire in its various forms.

[17] A practitioner who asks for and obtains food and welfare from

(continued...)

"Leaving one's homeland accomplishes half of the dharma", as is said so, leaving behind our homeland, we should wander unknown countries. Take leave of relatives and friends and, after you have done that, do not listen to their requests to put off the pursuit of dharma. Give away your wealth and possessions as gifts, then for livelihood, rely on whatever alms come your way.

We should recognize the entirety of sensuality as an obstacle come from having slipped into a bad habit and develop a mind set in which we do not care for it. For wealth and possessions too, if we do not develop a mind that is satisfied with whatever little does come along, anything we get will lead to wanting something more which is no different from being taken over by the mara of seductive sensuality.

No matter what good or bad talk is said about us, rather than taking it to be real, becoming filled with hope and fear over it, and attempting to stop whatever bad or promote whatever good talk has been said, we should leave it as totally all right, just as we would with talk about a person who has already died.

---

[17](...continued)
others so that he can do his practice, retreat, etcetera, must be a true practitioner, that is, one who is free from the eight worldly dharmas. Otherwise, harbouring the eight dharmas in the mind and just making yourself look like a dharmic person then asking for and obtaining the necessary requisites for practice is nothing short of wrong livelihood.

Except for a qualified guru, no-one, even our own father and mother, will give us advice that is truly straight so we should keep our own counsel and not give in to letting ourselves be led around by others.

Showing a tolerant disposition, we should be congenial, thinking of them as friends rather than treating everyone rudely, with hostility. And, if some of them do turn into obstructors of our practice, no matter how influential they might be, we should not allow them the power to move us; we should be like an boulder of iron with length of silk material attached. Then we will not be the kind of person who is easily moved by others, the type whose head turns this way and that like a treetop bending one way then another as the prevailing wind changes direction.

Whatever practice we do to gain accomplishment, we should go through with it from the time we start until the time we reach the end and, no matter what happens—whether lightning strikes from above, or the sea surges up from below, or rocks tumble down from the side, or death arrives—with the thought, "How could I break my commitment?", carry on with our oaths exactly as we made them until the end is reached. During the periods of meditation, sleep, and even during meal breaks, and so on, we should from the outset not allow bad habits to creep in but step by step put ourselves into the way of practice. Especially, we should pursue our practice at an even pace, doing every exercise in virtue—both those with and without complexity[18]—when it should be done, never allowing for even a moment the irregularity of sometimes doing it and sometimes putting it aside in favour of ordinary matters.

At the time of retreat, whether the doorway has been sealed with mud[19] or not, we should not meet others face to face, nor speak with them, nor look out for them. We should relax, putting aside all the distractions that come from mind worrying itself about this and that, then we should expel the stale airs, take up the key points of body properly, and then, leaving aside thinking mind in favour of a mindful awareness[20], plant mind so that, like an oaken stake, it does not move for even an instant[21]. These, which are the excellences of outer,

---

[18] Complexity can mean both involved with a lot of detail versus those that are simple, and also involved with mental activity versus those without.

[19] So that others cannot come in no matter what.

[20] It has become popular to translate "rigpa" with awareness but that is a very bad translation that shows no understanding of what rigpa actually is. In this book "awareness" is always used to translate Tib. shes which is the general term for the mere registering capacity of mind, that is, "awareness", whether as dualistic consciousness or non-dualistic wisdom. Here the author is using it to mean the consciousness in general of mind.

[21] Oak was one of the hardest woods known in Tibet. The image of an oaken stake conveys the sense of something that is so firm that it is totally immobile.

inner, and secret retreat, are the source from which all signs and good qualities[22] quickly arise.

Perhaps[23], because of some urgent matter, we could decide to meet someone and also talk with him. After doing so we might think, "I will be strict from now on", but the consequence of this sort of thing is that, having already fallen over the precipice, down into the abyss far away from practice, we will become more and more lax. Thus, from the very beginning, if we make a strict decision to stay put in the retreat, we will become stronger and stronger[24] and our practice will not be carried away by obstacles.

Many texts about examining the special signs of a place[25] have appeared but, generally speaking, any place which has been blessed by the presence of a siddha, such as Guru Rinpoche or others, and which is not frequented by samaya breakers, and also any place which is very isolated yet is one where necessities can easily be obtained, and so on, one that fits with one's own constitution[26], will be suitable.

---

[22] Signs of progress on the path and good qualities of being, all of which are developed by doing the practice.

[23] ... after having entered into the retreat as just mentioned.

[24] ... as the retreat progresses ...

[25] ... which indicate whether or not it is a suitable location for making a retreat ...

[26] ... mental and physical ...

There are also places such as charnel grounds and wild, harsh places inhabited by malevolent locale owners[27]. If we can quickly create an auspicious conjunction of events inner and outer and bring these spirits under control by means of our own powers[28], such places can be of great value to our meditation. On the other hand, if we cannot, there will be many obstacles. When adverse conditions such as these can be taken into our space of realization, they all change to appearing as our assistants, so, if we are capable in that way it will be really excellent for us to do the practice of the secret[29] in such places as cremation grounds.

The true meaning of isolation is to continually abstain from all entertaining activities, outer and inner, and so remain totally un-occupied.

The actual training of the mindstream is to exert ourselves in the common practices of the four mind reversers and the uncommon practices of taking refuge, cleansing obscuration,

---

[27] Tib. gzhi bdag. Locale owners are spirits who, literally, have claimed the place as their own turf. They regard themselves as the owners of the place and can be very dangerous if their turf is invaded by us for whatever reason.

[28] A yogin uses various means to turn a situation without welcome into one that is good for all concerned. This is usually done with outer ritual and inner mental approach both directed at transforming the situation in to an auspicious one.

[29] Usually translated as "secret practice" it means the practice of the secret, that is, Vajra Vehicle.

and accumulating accumulations[30]. We must exert ourselves at each one of these practices in the way laid out in the instruction manuals and must do so until experience has been brought forth for each. And, especially, we must be diligent at guru yoga until we have gained experience of this vital essence of the practice; if we don't, our meditation will only come to life slowly and, even if it does come on a little, obstructors will arise with it and a genuine realization will not arise in the mindstream. Thus, we should supplicate the guru with uncontrived, intense devotion. At some point because of that, there will be a transference to us of the understanding of his enlightened mindstream and because of that, a special realization which cannot be expressed in words will be born within us, it is certain. Lama Zhang Rinpoche[31] said,

> "There are many admonitions such as "preserve the abiding", "preserve the experience", "preserve the samadhi", and so on but this realization being born within through the blessings of the guru that come through the power of devotion is rare."

Therefore, given that the birth in our own mindstreams of Great Completion's meaning comes about through the agency of the preliminary practices, the Lord Drigungpa said,

> "Other dharmas make the main part out as the
> profound part;

---

[30] The first three of the four uncommon preliminary practices, the fourth being guru yoga which he emphasizes following this.

[31] A great Kagyu guru who was one of the disciples of Phagmo Drupa and founder of one of the four great and eight lesser lineages of the Kagyu.

> Here, I make out the preliminaries as the profound
> part."

and I also think that to be the case[32]!

---

[32] It is not uncommon for teachers to point out that the preliminary practices, made of the four common and four uncommon ones just described, are in fact the really profound practice. Doing so emphasizes the fact that these practices, when properly done, actually change your mind and do get you in touch with actuality.

MAIN PART: SEVERING THE EXAGGERATIONS OF VIEW, MEDITATION, AND CONDUCT AND ENTERING THE NARROW AVENUE OF PRACTICE

To begin with in the main part, there is the view. The view is a direct knowledge of what is. It is like this.

One's own mindness, the superfactual innate character's actuality, is determined on the basis of rigpa'ing freed of all conventions—the conceptual tokens produced through the rational mind's process of manufacture and manipulation—and through that rigpa shines forth nakedly as self-arising wisdom[33]. There is no expressing it in words, there is no

---

[33] Paraphrase: One's own mindness is not the surface, complex apparatus of dualistic mind but the very core of that dualistic mind, which is what mind is at root. One's own mindness is not other than one's own innate character, what one really is. That innate character is the actuality of all things, how things actually are, before any process of ignorance masks it. It is the superfactual situation, not the fictional situation. The way to arrive at or to determine it in actual experience is to find the knowing core of mind which is the mind of a buddha. That core is called "rigpa"

(continued...)

illustrating it by an example. Going into samsara, it is not worsened; going into nirvana, it is not bettered. It does not experience[34] birth; it does not experience cessation. It does not experience liberation; it does not experience confusion. It does not experience existence; it does not experience non-existence. It never has any delimitations; it never falls into any side. In short, because primordially it never comes into existence as something comprised of the conceptual tokens that elaborate phenomena, it is the essence alpha purity, the great, all-pervasive emptiness. And, the complexion of that emptiness being un-stopped, there are the dharmas of samsara and nirvana in their oceans of realms, self-appearing like the sun and the rays of the sun. So, because it has never

---

[33](...continued)
in Tibetan and "vidyā" in Sanskrit. It means the pure, dynamic sight of things by mind without any coverings or obscurations. The things that obscure or cover mind are the conceptual structures that function as the name cards within dualistic perception and which are called conceptual tokens. They are a product of the general process of dualistic mind which always either manufactures concepts about what is in front of it or alters what is in front of it to suit its conceptual needs. If you rid yourself totally of dualistic mind, you rid yourself of the whole conceptual process of perception, including the manufacturing and altering, and the tokens which are the whole key to the process. By doing that, you get right to rigpa itself and, if you do have a direct experience of that, you actually do have a direct experience in that moment of the wisdom of a buddha's mind seen nakedly ...

[34] Tib. myong ba. Literally "experienced" and meaning that the quality mentioned has never occurred to the rigpa. It has just never happened for it.

experienced an empty part which is a dead, flat expanse of nothing whatsoever, it is the nature, wisdom, the qualities, the great spontaneous existence. When this rigpa of appearance-emptiness unified like that—the personage of the three kaya's being, the primordial innate character's actuality—which itself is what is[35], is recognized just as it is, then that is called "the view beyond rational mind, of Great Completion". The great acharya[36] said,

"Beyond rational mind, dharmakaya, suchness …"

With that, we have made the mind[37] of Samantabhadra blaze forth for us in direct perception and what could be more enjoyable? This itself is the heart of the six million, four hundred thousand tantras of Great Completion, which are the ultimate all of the eighty-four thousand dharma heaps distinguished by the Conqueror. There is no more celestial

---

[35] This "what is" relates back to the "what is" in the second sentence of this paragraph. He started the section by saying that the view is what is so he now connects the view that he has introduced his disciples to back to that original summation of what the view is.

[36] Padmasambhava.

[37] Here, although the word mind is used, it means the enlightened operation of mind, not the samsaric one. You can tell this in the Tibetan because the word used is the honorific form of the usual word for samsaric mind.

destination than this. It is this which must be used as the basis for deciding all dharmas[38].

❀ ❀ ❀

Now, having internally severed doubts and exaggerations in relation to that view, the preservation of its continuity is called "meditation". All the other types of meditation having a focus[39] are conceptual types of meditation done by rational mind; that is not our way, it is not what we do! What we do is to put ourselves in the state in which that very view just mentioned has been planted and not lost, while allowing all of the awarenesses[40] of the five doors to be relaxed into being

---

[38] This is the ultimate reality and as such, if any decisions are to be made about any dharma—what it is, what its status is, and so on—this is what has to be the reference point for making that decision. In other texts, one would say that "emptiness" or some other philosophical idea would have to be used for this purpose. Here, he has introduced his disciples to this enlightened mind in their own, direct experience, and is saying to them, this, the thing which you actually experience as your own enlightenment is the very final reference for reality, not some philosophical or meditated-upon concept. It perhaps does not sound like much but his words are very beautiful and meaningful.

[39] Tib. gtad so. A focus is something that is only found in dualistic mind. It is a concept that dualistic mind is using as its reference for understanding whatever it is that it is cogitating over.

[40] See earlier footnote regarding awareness. Here the author is using it to mean the dualistic awareness that forms the conscious-

(continued...)

themselves and hence free of alteration. This is not meditation done so that you can say, "This is it!" If you meditate that way, it is rational mind, thus there is no meditation to be done; at the same time, you do not allow yourself to be distracted from it for even a moment. You put yourself right on who you are[41] and then, because becoming distracted from that is actual confusion[42], stay un-distracted from it. Whatever concept shines forth is put into rigpa shining forth and you do not follow after it nor do you attempt to stop it. "Well then", you say, "How do we do it?" All appearances, however an object shines forth into appearance, are treated the same: not falling into grasping at them as items of appearance, similar to a child looking inside a temple, they are left in freshness whereby every dharma appears each in its own place without corruption due to manufacture, without change of colour, without loss of brilliance, but unspoiled by grasping concepts that would cling to it, so all known appearance shine forth as naked luminosity-emptiness wisdom.

In general, the many different names that there are for the profound and likewise for the vast confuse all those of lesser understanding so I will show the meaning by pointing it out

---

[40](...continued)
ness of the five senses of a human.

[41] The text says "yourself" literally but it means yourself which is the innate character of every being, and which is directly experienced as the view that he has just shown his disciples.

[42] Here, confusion means the fundamental confusion which goes with the fundamental not rigpa'ing of samsara. In other words, he is saying, "actual samsara". See confusion in the glossary.

in one pithy ball. In between one thought that has ceased and the next that has not yet shone forth, there is a present awareness fresh and utterly unchanged, unmodified, a naked, illuminative knowing[43], isn't there? Yes, well, just that is how rigpa stays present in itself. And, thought comes again; you do not stay there forever in that state of suchness but another discursive thought suddenly shines forth, doesn't it? That is that rigpa's self-liveliness. Nonetheless, if you do not recognize it as such immediately it shines forth, then it will autonomously continue on its way as discursive thought, and that, called "chain of confusion", is the root of samsara. Merely by recognizing such thoughts immediately they shine forth, they do not continue on as such and, if you then just put yourself at rest on top of them, every discursive thought that shines forth will be vast open liberation in the experiential space of rigpa dharmakaya; just exactly this is the actual practice of Thorough Cut's view and meditation wrapped into one. Garab Dorje said,

> "From state of the expanse pure from the outset,
> Rigpa flashes forth in an instant of thought;
> It is like getting a jewel from the depths of the ocean,
> The dharmakaya not altered, not created by anyone."

This is where bone meets rock; it is necessary to meditate undistractedly night and day so please take every bit of your

---

[43] Tib. gsal rig. This term is used to define mind. Here it is used in the sense of "not just an ordinary, dualistic, illuminative knowing (which is mind by definition) but a an unmodified, naked, etc., kind of one, which is none other than rigpa".

theoretical knowledge of emptiness and pile it up on yourself in the form of rigpa!

❀ ❀ ❀

Now for that meditation, there are the two points: the way to extract profit through conduct; and the way to enter the narrow avenue of practice. The principal thing, as explained earlier, is to supplicate from your heart, like driving in a stake, the guru who you never separate for a moment from seeing as the buddha in person. This is called "devotion, the good cure all" because it is superior to all methods whatever they might be for removing obstructors and for extracting profit. It comes out to being the king of all methods.

As for the faults of meditation, if there is sinking and dullness, the rigpa should be invigorated; if there is production of thought causing agitation, the awareness should be relaxed. Then, when the meditation is going along, there is no need to use a restrictive mindfulness in order to contain the flickerings of the thought process of that which is meditating. Instead, use the mindfulness simply of not forgetting one's own face recognizing itself to preserve all activities—eating, sleeping, going, and staying—in any situation of equipoise and post-attainment as a continuous stream of it[44]. And, all of whatever shines forth—thoughts of happiness and sorrow, and of the afflictions—definitely should not be dealt with through hope and fear, rejection and adoption, something to

---

[44] It here means the meditation, which is in itself the state of being in rigpa.

be overcome via an antidote and the like, rather you put yourself in its essence just exactly as it presents itself—pleasant or unpleasant feeling or whatever—the essence being naked, wide-awake, and totally obvious.

For everything[45] there is nothing other than this one key point[46] so there is no need to spin your head with a lot of ideas[47]. Meditation in which emptiness is used as a separate antidote that is applied on top of discursive thoughts and afflictions seen as something to be abandoned is not necessary; at the same time as the thing to be abandoned is identified by rigpa, it goes into self-liberation, like a snake uncoiling itself. The majority of people know how to talk about this, the ultimate of hidden meanings of Luminosity Vajra Heart[48] but, not knowing the practice of it, they sit there just parroting away about it. Our[49] merit is very great indeed[50].

---

[45] … that could come up in your experience …

[46] … needed to deal with it …

[47] … about all different kinds of meditation and practices needed to deal with all the different facets of experience that might arise.

[48] Luminosity Vajra Heart is another name for the innermost level of Great Completion teaching. It is about luminosity and it is the very vajra core of one's being.

[49] Meaning him and his disciples to whom he has just shown the secret but that extends to anyone who does know how to do this practice.

[50] … because we have the great fortune of actually being able to do it …

There is still more to be carefully considered and understood. Throughout our succession of lives, from time without beginning until now, the primary enemy who has been binding us into samsaric existence is this pair grasped-grasping[51]. This time, due to the guru's kindness we have been introduced to the dharmakaya that dwells within us, and that consumes the pair of them like bird's down burned up fire vanishes without trace, without remainder; that is satisfying to the heart, isn't it? Now, having obtained the profound oral instructions for a quick path like this, not to practise them would be like putting a wish-granting gem into the mouth of a corpse! Oh my what a loss that would be! So, do not let your heart rot but get on with the practice!

Also, for beginners, the hollow chatter of bad discursive thoughts can cause mindfulness to be lost and the appearance of an undercurrent of many chains of discursive thoughts. When that discursive thought subsides and a wide-awake mindfulness arrives again, the practitioners sometimes have regret with the thought, "I am wandering". At that time though, they should not try at all to sever the discursive thoughts that were previously bothering them, nor should they develop regret, and so on over the distraction that has occurred, instead, when the wide-awake mindfulness does arrive again, it is enough just to preserve a continuity of things left settled into themselves right on the basis of that very mindfulness[52].

---

[51] See the glossary.

[52] In other words, the special type of mindfulness, a non-concep-

(continued...)

The saying, "See discursive thoughts as dharmakaya, do not reject them!" is very famous but, for as long as the energy of vipashyana has not been perfected, if, you put yourself into blank[53] shamatha just believing it to be a state which "is the dharmakaya all right", then you are probably putting yourself into a kind of equanimity in which there is none of the knowing that knows, "What is this? It is this", an equanimity whose style is indeterminate[54]. Therefore, from the first, look directly at whatever discursive thought shines forth then, not investigating it or researching it at all, rest right on the recognizer of the discursive thought itself, and, in the same manner as an old man watches children playing games, set yourself on that while not seeing them as important, not evaluating them, not developing ideas about them in any way. If you set yourself on it like that, then, whenever the conceptless abiding in which mind has been left to settle into being itself starts to move out, at the same time the occurrence that

---

[52](...continued)
tual mindfulness, is enough; just use that to preserve the practice of being in reality, a practice in which, as earlier explained, one allows things to settle into being what they really are, without any of the conceptual approach of alteration and construction being used.

[53] Tib. had po. This term means a blank state. It is usually pejorative and is so here. It means a stupid state of meditation in which you have gone into a nice cocoon. To do that, you have to drop the knowing aspect of mind and you become stupid in doing so.

[54] Tib. lung ma bstan. This state of mind is neither definitely virtuous nor definitely non-virtuous, it could be either, depending on what you do with it.

has suddenly started up also falls apart and in that moment wisdom beyond mind[55] shines forth nakedly and totally obvious.

Now while you are on the path, it will happen that this[56] will become mixed with some form of the three temporary experiences—bliss, clarity, and no thought—so when that does happen, rest without a whisker of the hope and fear that believes in and grasps at these as special attainments and just that will cut the possibility of the experience turning into a sidetrack.

It is important to do the meditation by continuously abandoning distraction, which is done by having a one-pointed intention to be mindful. If you do not have that and so go back and forth between resting in the state[57] and intellectual comprehension[58], you could develop the complacency of being proud of your mere beginnings of the shamatha side of practice. With that, you would not be honing your experi-

[55] As mentioned earlier, here "mind" means "samsaric mind".

[56] ... your state of practice of rigpa ...

[57] ... of rigpa ...

[58] Intellectual comprehension here refers to intellectual or theoretical-only understanding of Great Completion as opposed to actually being able to rest in the state of rigpa. Padmasaṃbhava taught comprehension, experience, and realization as three steps of the practice and the author is using that presentation here to make his point. You will see the three lines related to the three things explained over the course of the next two pages.

ence[59] and the mere expertise that you might have of being able to explain it verbally and put it into words will not be of any real help. As it says in Great Completion,

"Comprehension is like a patch, it falls away."

and,

"Experience is like mist, it dissolves away."

Accordingly, if even little conditions of the object, good and bad, deceive the meditator, there will be a great deal of disturbance for him due to conditions.

Even if you have developed the ability to have a stream of meditation, if you do not meditate steadily, then all the profound oral instructions will be left behind on the pages of your texts. A genuine meditation will never be produced by someone who has become resistant to clear thinking, resistant to dharma, and resistant to practice. A meditator who has not done his meditation for a very long time and who attempts to start it up afresh has the danger of dying with his brain encrusted with salt therefore we all have to be very careful about this point.

If you do this kind of familiarization over long period of time, then eventually, due to some appropriate condition such as devotion, etcetera, your experience will leap up into realization and you will see rigpa naked and obvious. Like removing a hood from your head, your experience of it will shift to

---

59 ... where experience is the next step and is desirable because it is an actual step towards final realization ...

being vast and wide open. That is called, "Not seeing which is the best seeing". From here on discursive thoughts will shine forth as meditation; abiding and movement will go on to liberation in the same moment. Moreover, that will occur in these steps: first, by recognizing discursive thought it is liberated, like meeting a person you have been acquainted with before; in the middle, discursive thought itself liberates itself, like a snake uncoiling; and finally, discursive thoughts are liberated without having any effect either helpful or harmful, like a thief who enters an empty house. After the third has happened, a very strong trust that comes from having decided that all dharmas are the magical display of self-knowing rigpa alone is born within. Waves of compassion rise up on emptiness. Making a choice between samsara and nirvana ends. There is the realization that there is no good and bad in being a buddha and a sentient being. Whatever else happens, there is no shifting from being only within a happy mind, the state of dharmatā, so there is, night and day without interruption, being which is an infinite expanse; as is said in Great Completion,

> "Realization is like space, it is without change.[60]"

For the yogin who has arrived at this level, even though his body appears to be that of an ordinary man, his mind has become that of the dharmakaya freed of all conceptual efforts, so he traverses every one of the grounds and paths without doing anything. In the end, his rational mind is exhausted

---

[60] This and the two preceding lines quoted from Padmasambhava are part of a very famous four line verse that shows the differences between theoretical understanding, temporary experience, and realization.

and dharmas are exhausted so, like the space within a vase that has been shattered, his body dissipates into subtle atoms and mind dissipates into dharmatā[61]. There will be what is called "pooling back into the primordial ground expanse, internal luminosity, the youthful vase body", won't there? There will, and since that is view, meditation, and conduct taken to the end, it is called "the fruition in which nothing has been attained is manifested".

Those levels of experience and realization furthermore arise both in a sequential progression and in a sudden occurrence which has no sequence to it. The latter belongs to a person of very special faculties but at the time of their respective fruitions, no distinction between the two can be made.

[61] Tib. chos nyid. Dharmatā is a term that is used to refer to the reality of any given situation. Here is refers to the reality within dualistic mind, which turns out to be the underlying reality of all phenomena.

POST-ATTAINMENT: PRESERVING SAMAYA AND INCLUDING THIS LIFE'S ACTIVITIES WITHIN DHARMA

Even though you might have exerted yourself at the practice like that of view, meditation, and conduct, your vows and samaya[62] could degenerate because of not being skilled in post-attainment's activities. If that happens, along the way there will be obstructors to the attainment of the levels and paths and there will be obstacles in general, and ultimately, it is certain that you will fall into the hell of unremitting torment, Avichi. Therefore, it is absolutely important that anything you do is, through never being separated from the watchman of mindful awareness, always connected to unmistaken adoption and rejection. The great āchārya[63] said,

> "Overall, your view might be loftier than the sky but
> Your karmic cause and effect must also be finer
> than flour."

---

[62] Vows refers to the vows of the Lesser and Great Vehicles and samaya to the vows of the Vajra Vehicle.

[63] Padmasambhava.

In view of that, that you should abandon the coarse mind that goes along in a blank, uncomprehending state and conduct yourself with precision and in relation to cause and effect.

Vows including samayas should be kept without the tiniest infraction so that you are not stained by faults and downfalls. There are many enumerations of the secret mantra samayas but, if they are summed up, they come down to the samayas of the root guru's enlightened body, speech, and mind. It is said that, "The perception for as much as a moment that the guru is an ordinary man delays accomplishment by years and months". Why is that so? It is because of the key point of severity of the object,

> "It is so because the vajra holders have said
> Accomplishment follows on from the master."

In view of that, it is true for anyone that, until the time he has initially accepted someone as guru, he is free to do as he pleases but, once he has accepted that person as guru and become connected through the empowerments and oral instructions, he has no choice but to keep the samayas. At the conclusion of the fourth empowerment, you bow before the guru, the chief of the mandala, and say,

> "Starting from today I am your servant;
> I offer myself to you so
> Please accept me as your disciple and
> Use even a part of me ..."

and having made that declaration, you are then, no matter how great or powerful you might be, under the yoke of the guru, aren't you? Similarly, once you have committed yourself with,

> "Whatever the leader commands
> All that I will do[64] ..."

are you in a position henceforth not to do what you are told? If you do not do what you have committed to with those words, you are not worthy of being called anything but "samaya corruptor", even if it is not a nice name to hear.

Furthermore, some have the idea that a person should take extra care over keeping their samaya with great gurus who have a large following and who are rich, powerful, and very capable but that it is not necessary to guard the samaya with lesser, apparently inferior, gurus who keep the yogic discipline of being poor and unpretentious. There is simply no explanation of such a thing! There has to be an understanding in every case of the key issue of the risks involved with the rewards. Anyone who does not have that understanding will be stuck like a old horse who has no idea of the way, and it will not work out for that person.

In order to guard the samaya properly like that, you need to give whatever you do—whether it is for the guru or for yourself—your full attention and consideration, like when grinding and preparing medicine. If you are doing something for the guru, do it carefully for as long as it takes and that, of

---

[64] ... which is the other main verse said at the conclusion of an empowerment in relation to accepting the samaya and command of the guru who has given the empowerment ...

course, will be good. Even if you are doing something for yourself, it makes no sense to throw ashes on your own head!

Then in terms of the samayas themselves, there is the close associates' samaya. In general, you should look very favourably on everyone who has entered the door of the Buddha's teaching and you should train in sacred outlook towards them, giving up all sectarianism, denigration, and so on. In particular, for all of those who are your vajra relatives because of having the same guru and having been together in the same empowerment mandala, you must give up on treating them with contempt, competitiveness, envy, deceit, and so on and, from your heart, be loving and respectful towards them.

Meditate on unbearable compassion thinking, "All sentient beings at some time or another have been my own, exceptionally caring parents but, now, good grief, these very beings are afflicted with the intense suffering of a cyclic existence from which they cannot escape. If I do not protect them, who will?", and do your Mind Training[65]. All in all, use your three doors as much as you possibly can only to accomplish the welfare of beings and dedicate all of your merit for the sake of others. There are three things to keep in mind continuously—dharma, guru, and sentient beings—and nothing else; if you do that, your thoughts and practices will not become scattered.

---

[65] Tib. blo sbyong. Mind Training does not mean mind training in general but is the name of one of two specific ways for developing the enlightenment mind (bodhichitta). The development of enlightenment mind is an essential part of the practice. This sentence and the next join together.

Do not try to compete with those who have either signs of progress or are said to be realized nor with monastic types, instead keep your mouth shut and your thoughts under control. Just this is singularly important so do not act stupidly or deceitfully.

When it says in the foundations of dharma, "Thinking of one's own purpose in regard just to future lives"[66], it means that dharma is something that we do have to practise ourselves. We could put our hopes in roots of merit made by others for us after we have died but it is very difficult for that to be of benefit[67]. In view of that, you should draw your mind inwards and first go through the preparatory practices that set

---

[66] When the path of practice of Buddhism is set out in general, the very first step is for a person to stop thinking about this life and to start thinking for his own purposes about where he will be going in future lives. After that, he could think for his own purposes of getting out of samsara all together. Finally, he could think for the purpose of all others of going to truly complete enlightenment. Therefore, for this first level of thought, it is "thinking of one's own purpose and *just* in regard to future lives".

[67] It is a common way of thinking in the tradition of Buddhism that, when a person has just died, the living should undertake virtuous actions and dedicate the merit accumulated back to the dying person because, theoretically, it could help the person on the journey through the intermediate state. However, in reality, it is very difficult to help a person who has died that way. Therefore, he is saying here that any of us should not even think to rely on a method like that but should get on with our own dharma practice here and now and prepare for our own future by our own efforts.

a foundation. The foundation is the development of a heartfelt renunciation that causes very strong perseverance driven by the decision that one's life will be none other than practice. Then, for the main part, press the key points of the practice of profound view and meditation and, in post-attainment, conduct yourself within the vows of samaya and of training[68] in a way that is not contrary to adoption and rejection. In the wake of this approach, good qualities will uncontrollably arise from the inside because Great Completion is a path that forces[69] buddhahood to come on even for those who have accumulated evil.

The intense profundity contained in this Great Completion can also bring on obstacles, as the great risks that accompany great rewards. The reason for it is that all of one's previously accumulated bad karma is ripened by the potency of the oral instructions and signs of that do appear. Externally, mara obstacles could arise as apparitional occurrences: in the place of practice, they might appear in the forms of gods and demons and they might call you by name and falsely appear as the guru and give you the prophecy[70]; and various fearful

---

[68] The vows of samaya are the vows of the Vajra Vehicle and the vows of training, as before, are the vows of the Lesser and Great Vehicles.

[69] Meaning to force an issue and hence make something come on quickly. For example, like yelling in the ear of a sleeping person forces them to wake up and all of a sudden, too.

[70] All of this could happen and, despite any mental or physical damage that might go with it, your innate mind cannot be harm-

(continued...)

apparitions could occur in experiences or dreams. Then, also for actual occurrences, various unspecified things such as others hitting and beating you, attacks of robbers and thieves, sickness, and so on, could occur. And, in relation to mind, you might experience intense suffering for no reason; you could be depressed and want to burst in tears; there might be intense afflictions, accompanied by a diminishing of your devotion, bodhichitta, and compassion; and discursive thoughts rising up as enemies could start to drive you mad; and you could misunderstand talk intended to help; and, losing all desire to stay in the mountains, you might feel deeply as though you want to give up on your commitment to it; and wrong views regarding the guru could arise; and doubts and so forth towards the dharma might arise. Then, coming from others, there can be false accusations of wrong-doing, bad talk leading to a bad reputation, friends turning into enemies, and so on. All in all, it is possible that various unwanted conditions, inner and outer, will arise. Yes, well, all this is part of how it comes out, so it should be recognized!

All of the risks and rewards are contained within that. Moreover, if you deal with those obstacles via the key points, they will be transformed into accomplishment, and if you fall under their influence, they will become obstructors. In regard to this, as a person whose determination is built on pure samaya and nothing less than total devotion, surrender to the guru, give him your heartfelt trust, and whatever your

[70](...continued)
ed by it so there is only one thing to do and that is to do the practice of recognizing the nature of mind behind all the appearance. That is the one way to deal with all of it.

actions, supplicate him like planting a stake. Let those bad conditions fuel your desire to continue and make intense efforts at practice and then, at some point, the condition whatever it is, having been allowed to assert itself, will naturally fall away and, having departed, will turn out to have been profitable to your practice. Appearances do just fade away but, when tempered by the guru and his oral instructions, they can also turn into something worthwhile. After that has been accomplished, henceforth, they do continue to impose themselves but you now approach them through an assurance you have discovered that thinks, "Ah yes, there you are!", and that finishes it up; these conditions are now turning into the path so it is just fine for them to arise and do what they do. A la la, how wonderful! This is it; just exactly what our old fathers wanted for us! All in all in relation to this, do not act like the fox who, wanting to eat, slyly steals towards a human corpse with knees trembling, rather, develop a strength of mind!

And then there are the types who have inferior accumulations of outflowed merit[71], who are loose in their samayas and vows, who have strong wrong views, have many doubts, and who make high promises but have feeble practice. Let them sit there with their stinky farts hanging over the guru's oral

---

[71] There are two kinds of merit: outflowed and un-outflowed. The former is made without a connection to wisdom and is much inferior to the latter which is made with wisdom. Here, he is saying, weak types of practitioners who are just like the ordinary people who accumulate just a little bit of merit and not only that but only accumulate the outflowed merit of beings caught in samsara.

instructions on the reading stand before them! When they are gripped by death, they will follow along after those bad conditions of theirs and mara will easily lead them down the path of rotten migration. Oh how horrible this is! Supplicate the guru that this sort of thing will not happen to you.

And moreover, transforming bad conditions into the path is relatively easy. However, transforming good conditions into the path is extremely difficult because practitioners can develop the pride of having high realization and having done so can become agents of the mara of the utterly distracted son of the gods whose every activity is nothing more than a method for greatness in this life, thus it requires extreme caution. Understand that this has in it a scale that shows whether the meditator is going up or down.

For as long as you have not perfected the ability that goes with the qualities of inner realization, it is not proper to give accounts of the heights of your experience to others, therefore keep quiet about it! Furthermore, instead of reminiscing over your great activity during months and years of hard retreat, apply yourself earnestly to practice with the intent that you will make the whole of your human life valuable! Do not be seduced by an intellect that speaks of emptiness into devaluing the practice of virtue that takes account of cause and effect at the fictional level! Do not stay long in village places doing rites for the villagers such as taming local demons for the sake of food! Reduce meaningless activity, unnecessary talk, and unhelpful mulling over of things! Fraud, deceptive practices, and so on are contrary to the dharma so do not involve yourself in tricking others! Attempting to get anything because of your attachment to sensual enjoyments through less than honest ways of talking, such as flattery, and so on, is wrong livelihood, so don't do it! Do not associate with those whose view and conduct do not fit with your own and who engage in bad actions. Expose your own faults to yourself; do not speak of other's faults. All types of tobacco have been stated to be a manifestation of Damsi demons[72] so should be wholeheartedly abandoned. Beer and the like are to be used as samaya substance but do not drink them without mindfulness just to become drunk.

The faithful behave respectfully, while the faithless denigrate others, make preparations for bad things, and so on. All you encounter should be taken onto the path without making a distinction between who is connected with good and bad and you should accept them all with pure prayers of aspiration. At all times, inwardly maintain an exalted state of heroic rigpa that does not shrink back while outwardly maintaining an unpretentious style of behaviour! Wear tattered clothing! Put all others whether they are good, bad, or in between, above yourself! Adopt a livelihood in which your basic needs are met and no more, then keep to staying in mountainous regions! Aim to lead the life of a beggar! Set the life stories of the forefather siddhas[73] as your example! How important it is not let the past take charge of your life but to make a fresh, clean start out of dharma! How important it is not to let current circumstances as they arrive take charge of your

---

[72] A kind of negative force or spirit that causes corruption of samaya.

[73] Accomplished ones.

life but, to stand firm in the face of whatever circumstance arises and be up to dealing with it!

In short, having set your own mind as the judge, wrap this human life of yours up into dharma so that, at the time of death, with nothing else left to be concerned about, you can die without embarrassment at what you have done! The key issue of all practice is contained in that, right there. Then, when the time of death does come, you will be able to give up whatever wealth and possessions you have without attachment and clinging to even a needle's worth of it[74].

Moreover, the best person has great joy at the point of death, the middling person has no worry at the point of death, and the least person dies but without regrets. Then, these types enter the state of the luminosity of realization around the clock, night and day, so they have no intermediate state and only the stamp of their body remains. If they cannot manage that but they do have assurance of liberation in the intermediate state, then whatever happens is fine. However, if that also is not the case, a practitioner should develop experience in transference[75] beforehand, then, connecting with that at the

---

[74] In Tibet, most people would have a needle and thread in their personal items, even poor people. Therefore, there was talk of not having attachment even to that little needle that you carried around with you.

[75] Tib. phowa practice, the practice of transferring the consciousness prior to the onset of the death process. The death process is regarded as a very difficult path for anyone to deal with, so if one doesn't have the capacity or doesn't think that one will accom-

(continued...)

time of death, he will be able to transfer himself to the field[76] of his preference and there traverse the remaining levels and paths to become a buddha.

So, this precious lineage of ours is not just an old story of the past; even today people go to the final realization of Thorough Cut and Direct Crossing, whereupon their material form passes into a rainbow body's mass of light, and it really does happen like this. Having found this gem you do not have to seek out some lesser trinket, rather, to have met with this sort of profound instruction like the heart's blood of the dakinis is extreme good fortune so you should take joy in and cultivate the glorified mind[77].

May this book be kept as a jewel next to the heart of my followers for by doing so, great benefit is possible.

---

[75](...continued)
plish it before death, one should practise transference to the point of proficiency. Then the death process can be by-passed.

[76] Tib. zhing khams. Meaning any of the several levels of enlightened field that there are. Doing this allows the practitioner in the bardo to go up to an enlightened level of existence where enlightened can easily be finalized rather than taking birth in samsara again with the much more difficult path to enlightenment entailed in that.

[77] The mind of the realization of Great Completion, which is glorified by all the beings who know of it as the supreme attainment.

With the main cause being my thoughts of the mountain dharma practice of the meditators at the meditation centre of Ogmin Padma Od Ling and the contributory condition being the request of the diligent meditator Rigzang Dorje who possesses the jewel of unfaltering faith and devotion, I, Jigdral Yeshe Dorje, expressed this in the form of an essential guidance that contains advice given as words from the heart. May it be the cause of rapid birth of realization of wisdom in the mindstreams of fortunate ones.

Translated by Lotsawa Tony Duff in Swayambunath, Nepal, April, 2007. May there be goodness!

GLOSSARY

Actuality, Tib. gnas lugs: A key term in both sutra and tantra and one of a pair of terms, the other being apparent reality (Tib. snang lugs). The two terms are used when determining the reality of a situation. The actuality of any given situation is how (lugs) the situation actuality sits or is present (gnas); the apparent reality is how any given situation appears to an observer. Something could appear in many different ways, depending on the circumstances at the time and on the being perceiving it but, regardless of those circumstances, it will always have its own actuality, how it really is. The term actuality is frequently used in Mahāmudrā and Great Completion teachings to mean the fundamental reality of any given phenomenon or situation before any deluded mind alters it and makes it appear differently.

Affliction, Skt. kleśha, Tib. nyon mongs: This term is usually translated as emotion or disturbing emotion, etcetera but Buddha was very specific about the meaning of this word. When the Buddha referred to the emotions, meaning a movement of mind, he did not refer to them as such but called them "kleśha" in Sanskrit, meaning exactly "affliction". It is a basic part of the Buddhist teaching that emotions afflict beings, giving them problems at the time and causing more problems in the future.

Alpha purity, Tib. ka dag: A Great Completion term meaning purity that is there from the first, that is, primordial purity. There are many terms in Buddhism that express the notion of "primordial purity" but this one is unique to the Great Completion teaching. Some people do not like the term "alpha purity" but this is exactly what the Tibetan says.

Alteration, altered, same as contrivance q.v.

Assurance, Tib. gdeng: Although often translated as confidence, this term means assurance with all of the extra meaning conveyed by that term. A bird might be confident of its ability to fly but more than that, it has the assurance that it will not fall to the ground because of knowing that it has wings and the training to use them. Similarly, a person might be confident that they could liberate the afflictions but not assured of doing so because of lack of training or other causes. However, a person who has accumulated the causes to be able to liberate afflictions trained is assured of the ability to do so.

Clarity or Illumination, Skt. vara, Tib. gsal ba: When you see this term, it should be understood as an abbreviation of the full term in Tibetan, 'od gsal ba, which is usually translated as luminosity. It is not another factor of mind distinct from luminosity but merely a convenient abbreviation in both Indian and Tibetan dharma language for the longer term, luminosity. See "Luminosity" in this glossary for more.

Clinging, Tib. zhen pa: In Buddhism, this term refers specifically to the twofold process of dualistic mind mis-taking things that are not true, not pure, as true, pure, etcetera and then, because of seeing them as highly desirable even though they are not, attaching itself to or clinging to those things. This type of clinging acts as a kind of glue that keeps you with the unsatisfactory things of cyclic existence because of mistakenly seeing them as desirable.

Complexion, Tib. mdangs: In both Mahāmudrā and Great Completion there is the general term "offput" (Tib. gdangs) meaning what is given off by something, for example the sound given off by a loudspeaker. There is another Tibetan word spelled "mdangs" instead of "gdangs". The Mahāmudrā teaching makes no difference between the two terms but Great Completion teachings does make a distinction. In great completion this term spelled "mdangs" has the special meaning not of the general output or offput coming from something but of the "complexion" of thing. It is a more subtle meaning. In Great Completion it conveys not just the sense of what is given off by the emptiness factor of mind in general (which would be its offput and which is talked about, too) but specifically means the complexion of the emptiness or, you could also say, its lustre.

Conceptual tokens, Tib. mtshan ma. Conceptual tokens are the actual structures or concepts that conceptual mind uses during the process of perception. For example, you could see a table in direct visual perception of table in which case there would be no conceptual tokens involved. Or, you could think "table" in a conceptual perception of table in which case there is a always a name-tag "table" used whenever the table is referenced. The name tag is the conceptual token. This term is often used in Buddhist literature as way of inferring that the process of mind being discussed is not one of non-dualistic wisdom but one of dualistic mind.

Confusion, Tib. 'khrul pa: In Buddhism, this term mostly refers to the fundamental confusion of taking things the wrong way that happens because of fundamental ignorance though it can also have the more general meaning of having lots of thoughts and being confused about it. In the first case, it is defined like this, "Confusion is the appearance to rational mind of something being present when it is not", and refers for example to seeing an object, such as a table, as being truly present when in fact it is present only as mere, interdependent appearance.

Contrivance, contrived, Tib. bcos pa: A term meaning that something has been altered from its native state.

Cyclic existence, Skt. saṃsāra, Tib. 'khor ba: The type of existence that sentient beings have which is that they continue on from one existence to another, always within the enclosure of births that are produced by ignorance and experienced as unsatisfactory. Although the Tibetan term literally means "cycling", the original Sanskrit has a slightly different meaning; it means to go about, here and there.

Dharmakaya, Tib. chos sku: The mind of a buddha. Dharma here means reality, what actually is, and kāya means body.

Dharmata, Tib. chos nyid: A Sanskrit term used to refer to the reality of any given situation. Thus, there are many dharmatās. The term is often used in Buddhism to refer to general reality that underlies all types of existence but that is not its only meaning. For example, even the fact of water's wetness can be referred to as the dharmatā of water, meaning water's reality in general. The term is similar to "actuality" (Tib. gnas lugs).

Direct Crossing, Tib. tho rgal: The name of the two main practices of the innermost level of Great Completion. The other one is Thorough Cut.

Discursive thought, Skt. vikalpita, Tib. rnam rtog: This means more than just the superficial thought that is heard as a voice in the head. It includes the entirety of conceptual process that arises due to mind contacting any object of any of the senses. The Sanskrit and Tibetan literally mean "(dualistic) thought (that arises from the mind wandering among the) various (superficies perceived in the doors of the senses)".

Effort, Tib. rtsol ba: In Buddhism, this term usually does not merely mean effort but has the specific connotation of effort of dualistic mind. In that case, it is effort that is produced by and functions specifically within the context of dualistic concept. For example, the term "mindfulness with effort" specifically means "a type of mindfulness that is occurring within the context of dualistic mind and its various operations". The term "effortless" is often used in Mahāmudrā and Great Completion to mean a way of being in which dualistic mind has been abandoned and, therefore, has with it none of the effort of dualistic mind.

Elaboration, Tib. spro ba: to be producing thoughts.

Enlightenment mind, Skt. bodhicitta, Tib. byang chub sems: A key term of the Great Vehicle. It is the type of mind that is connected not with the lesser enlightenment of an arhat but the enlightenment of a truly complete buddha. As such, it is a mind that is connected with the aim of bringing all sentient beings to that same level of buddhahood. A person who has this mind has entered the Great Vehicle and is either a bodhisatva or a buddha.

It is important to understand that the term is used to refer equally to the minds of all levels of bodhisatva on the path to buddhahood and to the mind of a buddha who has completed the path. Therefore it is not "mind striving for enlightenment" as is so often translated but "enlightenment mind", that kind of mind which is connected with the full enlightenment of a truly complete buddha and which is present in all those who belong to the Great Vehicle. The term is used in the conventional Great Vehicle and also in the Vajra Vehicle. In the Vajra Vehicle, there are some special uses of the term where substances of the pure aspect of the subtle physical body are understood to be manifestations of enlightenment mind.

Entity, Tib. ngo bo: The entity of something is just exactly what that thing is. In English we would often simply say "thing" rather than entity but there is the problem that, in Buddhism, "thing" has a very specific meaning and not the general meaning that it has in English. See also under Essence in this glossary.

Equipoise and post-attainment, Tib. mnyam bzhag and rjes thob: Although often called "meditation and post-meditation", the actual term is "equipoise and post-attainment". There is great meaning in the actual wording which is lost by the looser translation.

Essence, Tib. ngo bo: This is a key term used throughout Buddhist theory. The original in Sanskrit and the term in Tibetan, too, has both meanings of "essence" and "entity". In some situations the term has more the first meaning and in others, the second. For example, when speaking of mind and mind's essence, it is referring to the core or essential part within mind. On the other hand, when speaking of something such as fire, one can speak of the entity, fire, and its characteristics, such as heat, and so on; in this case, the term does not mean essence but means that thing, what is actually is.

Exaggeration, Tib. skur 'debs pa: In Buddhism, this term is used in two ways. Firstly, it is used in general to mean misunderstanding from the perspective that one has added more to one's understanding of something than needs to be there. Secondly, it is used specifically to indicate that dualistic mind always overstates or exaggerates whatever object it is examining. Dualistic mind always adds the ideas of solidity, permanence, singularity, and so on to everything it references via the concepts that it uses. Severing of exaggeration either means removal of these un-necessary understandings when trying to properly comprehend something or removal of the dualistic process altogether when trying to get to the non-dualistic reality of a phenomenon.

Expanse, Skt. dhātu, Tib. dbyings: A Sanskrit term with over twenty meanings to it. Many of those meanings are also present in the Tibetan equivalent. In the Vajra Vehicle teachings it is used as a replacement for the term emptiness that conveys a non-theoretical sense of the experience of emptiness. When used this way, it has the sense "expanse" because emptiness is experienced as an expanse in which all phenomena appear.

Fictional, Skt. saṃvṛti, Tib. kun rdzob: This term is paired with the term "superfactual" q.v. Until now these two terms have been translated as "relative" and "absolute" but the translations are nothing like the original terms. These terms are extremely important in the Buddhist teaching so it is very important that they be corrected but more than that, if the actual meaning of these terms is not presented, then the teaching connected with them cannot be understood.

The Sanskrit term saṃvṛti means a deliberate invention, a fiction, a hoax. It refers to the mind of ignorance which, because of being obscured and so not seeing suchness, is not true but a fiction. The things that appear to the ignorance are therefore fictional. Nonetheless, the beings who live in this ignorance believe that the things that appear to them through the filter of ignorance are true, are real. Therefore, these beings live in fictional truth.

Fictional truth, Skt. saṃvṛtisatya, Tib. kun rdzob bden pa: See under "Fictional" for an explanation of this term.

Fortunate person, Tib. skal ldan: A person who has accumulated the karma needed to be involved with any given practice of dharma. This term is especially used in relation to the Vajra Vehicle whose practices are generally very hard to meet with. To meet with them, a person has to have developed all of the karma needed for such a rare opportunity, and this kind of person is then called "a fortunate one" or "fortunate person".

Grasped-grasping, Tib. gzung 'dzin: When mind is turned outwardly as it is in the normal operation of dualistic mind, it has developed two faces that appear simultaneously. Special names are given to these two faces: mind appearing in the form of the external object being referenced is called "that which is grasped". Mind appearing in the form of the consciousness that is referencing it is called "the grasper" or "grasping" of it. Thus, there is the pair of terms "grasped-grasper" or "grasped-grasping". When these two terms are used, it alerts you immediately to the fact that a Mind Only style of presentation is being discussed. This pair of terms pervades Mind Only, Madhyamaka, and tantric writings and is exceptionally important in all of them.

Note that you could substitute the word "apprehended" for "grasped" and "apprehender" for "grasper" or "grasping" and that would reflect one connotation of the original Indian terminology. The solidified duality of grasped and grasper is nothing but an invention of dualistic thought. It has that kind of character or characteristic.

Great Completion, rdzogs pa chen po: Two main practices of reality developed in the Buddhist traditions of ancient India and then came to Tibet: Great Completion (Mahāsaṅdhi) and Great Seal (Mahāmudrā). Great Completion and Great Seal are names for reality and names for a practice that directly leads to that reality. Their ways of describing reality and their practices are very similar. The Great Completion teachings are the pinnacle teachings of the tantric teachings of Buddhism that first came into Tibet with Padmasambhava and his peers and were later kept alive in the Nyingma (Earlier Ones) tradition. The Great Seal practice came into Tibet later and was held in the Sakya and Kagyu lineages. Later again, the Great Seal became held by the Gelugpa lineage, which obtained its transmissions of the instructions from the Sakya and Kagyu lineages.

These days it is popular to call Great Completion by the name Great Perfection. However, that is a mistake. The original name Mahāsaṅdhi means that one space of reality in which all things come together. Thus it means "completeness" or "completion" as the Tibetans chose to translate it and does not imply or contain the sense of "perfection".

Great Vehicle, Skt. mahāyāna, Tib. theg pa chen po: The Buddha's teachings as a whole can be summed up into three vehicles where a vehicle is defined as that which can carry you to a certain destination. The first vehicle, called the Lesser Vehicle, contains the teachings designed to get an individual moving on the spiritual path through showing the unsatisfactory state of cyclic existence and an emancipation from that. However, that path is only concerned with personal emancipation and fails to take account of all of the beings that there are in existence. There used to be eighteen schools of Lesser Vehicle in India but the only one surviving these days is the Theravada of south-east Asia. The Greater Vehicle is a step up from that. The Buddha explained that it was great in comparison to the Lesser Vehicle for seven reasons. The first of those is that it is concerned with attaining the truly complete enlightenment of a truly complete buddha for the sake of every sentient being where the Lesser Vehicle is concerned only with a personal liberation that is not truly complete enlightenment and which is achieved only for the sake of that practitioner. The Great Vehicle has two divisions. There is a conventional Great Vehicle in which the path is taught in a logical, conventional way. There is also an unconventional Great Vehicle in which the path is taught in an unconventional and very direct way. This latter vehicle is called the Vajra Vehicle because it takes the innermost, indestructible (vajra) fact of reality of one's own mind as the vehicle to enlightenment.

Ground, Tib. gzhi: This is the first member of the formulation of ground, path, and fruition. Ground, path, and fruition is the way that the teachings of the path of oral instruction belonging to the Vajra Vehicle are presented to students. Ground refers to the basic situation as it is.

Introduction and To Introduce, Tib. ngos sprad and ngos sprod pa respectively: This pair of terms is usually translated in the U.S.A. these days as "pointing out" "and "to point out" but this is a mistake that has, unfortunately, become entrenched. The terms are the standard terms used in day to day life for the situation in which one person introduces another person to someone or something. They are the exact same words as our English "introduction" and "to introduce".

In the Vajra Vehicle, these terms are specifically used for the situation in which one person introduces another person to the nature of his own mind. Now there is a term in Tibetan for "pointing out" but that term is never used for this purpose because in this case no-one points out anything. Rather, a person is introduced by another person to a part of himself that he has forgotten about.

Isness: A translation of dharmatā, q.v.

Key points, Tib. gnad: Key points are those places in one's being that one works, like pressing buttons, in order to get some desired effect. For example, in meditation, there are key points of the body; by adjusting those key points, the mind is brought closer to reality and the meditation is thus assisted.

In general, this term is used in Buddhist meditation instruction but it is, in particular, part of the special vocabulary of the Great Completion teachings. Overall, the Great Completion teachings are given as a series of key points that must be attended to in order to bring forth the various realizations of the path.

Lesser Vehicle, Skt. hīnayāna, Tib. theg pa dman pa: see under Great Vehicle.

Liveliness, Tib. rtsal: A key term in both Mahāmudrā and Great Completion. The term means the ability that something has to express itself. In the case of rigpa, it refers to how the rigpa actually comes out into expression. The term is sometimes translated as "display" but that is not right. It is not merely the display that is being talked about here but the fact that something has the ability to express itself in a certain way. Another English word that fits the meaning, though one which is much drier than "liveliness" is "expressivity". In the end, given the way that this term is actually used in the higher tantras, it refers to the liveliness of whatever is being referred to, usually rigpa.

Luminosity, Skt. prabhāsvara, Tib. 'od gsal ba: the core of mind, called mind's essence, has two aspects, parts, or factors as they are called. One is emptiness and the other is knowing. Luminosity is a metaphor for the fundamental knowing quality of the essence of mind. It is sometimes translated as "clear light" but that is a mistake that comes from not understanding how the words of the Sanskrit and the Tibetan, too, go together. It does not refer to a light that has the quality of clearness (something that makes no sense, actually!) but refers to the illuminative property which is the hallmark of mind. Mind knows, that is what it does. Metaphorically, it is a luminosity that illuminates its own content. In both Sanskrit and Tibetan Buddhist literature, the term is frequently abbreviated just to gsal ba, "clarity", with the same meaning.

Mara, Tib. bdud: a Sanskrit term closely related to the word "death". Buddha spoke of four classes of extremely negative influences that have the capacity to drag a sentient being deep into samsara. They are the "maras" or "kiss of death" of: having a samsaric set of five skandhas; of having afflictions; of death itself; and of the son of gods, which means being seduced and taken in totally by sensuality.

Mind, Skt. chitta, Tib. sems: the complicated process of mind which occurs because there is ignorance. This sort of mind is a samsaric phenomenon. It is a dualistic mind.

Mindfulness, Tib. dran pa: A particular mental event, one that has the ability to keep mind on its object. Together with alertness, it is one of the two causes of developing shamatha. See alertness for a explanation.

Mindness, Skt. chittatā, Tib. sems nyid. Mindness is a specific term of the tantras. It is one of many terms meaning the essence of mind or the nature of mind. It conveys the sense of "what mind is at its very core". It has sometimes been translated as "mind itself" but that is a misunderstanding of the Tibetan word "nyid". The term does not mean "that thing mind" where mind refers to dualistic mind. Rather, it means the very core of dualistic mind, what mind is at root, without all of the dualistic baggage.

Mindness is a path term. It refers to exactly the same thing as "actuality" or "actuality of mind" which is a ground term but does so from the practitioner's perspective. It conveys the sense to a practitioner that he might still have baggage of dualistic mind that has not been purified yet but there is a core to that mind that he can work with.

Not stopped, Tib. ma 'gags pa: An important path term in the teaching of both Mahāmudrā and Great Completion. The essence of mind has two parts: emptiness and luminosity. Both of these must come unified. However, when a practitioner does the practice, he will fall into one extreme or the other and that is called "stoppage". The aim of the practice is to get to the stage in which there is both emptiness and luminosity together. In that case, there is no stoppage of falling into one extreme or the other. Thus non-stopped luminosity is a term that indicates that there is the luminosity with all of its appearance yet that luminosity, for the practitioner, is not mistaken, is not stopped off. Stopped luminosity is an experience like luminosity but in which the appearances have, at least to some extent, not been mixed with emptiness.

Offput, Tib. gdangs: A general Tibetan term meaning that which is given off by something else, for example, the sound that comes from a loudspeaker. In Mahāmudrā and Great Completion, it the general term used to refer to what is given off by the emptiness factor of the essence of mind. Emptiness is the empty condition of the essence of mind, like space. However, that emptiness has liveliness and liveliness comes off it as compassion and all the other qualities of enlightened mind, and, equally, all the apparatus of dualistic mind. All of this collectively is called its offput. Note that the Great Completion teachings have a special word that is a more refined version of this term; see "complexion" for that.

Post-attainment, Tib. rjes thob: see "Equipoise and post-attainment".

Prajna, Tib. shes rab: A Sanskrit term for the type of mind that makes good and precise distinctions between this and that and hence which arrives at good understanding. It is sometimes translated as "wisdom" but that is not correct because it is, generally speaking, a mental event belonging to dualistic mind where "wisdom" is generally used to refer to the non-dualistic knower of a Buddha. Moreover, the main feature of prajna is its ability to distinguish correctly between one thing and another and hence to have a good understanding. It is very much part of intellect.

Preserve, Tib. skyong ba: An important term in both Mahāmudrā and Great Completion. In general, it means to defend, protect, nurture, maintain. In the higher tantras it means to keep something just as it is, to nurture that something so that it stays and is not lost. Also, in the higher tantras, it is often used in reference to preserving the state where the state is some particular state of being. Because of this, the phrase "preserve the state" is an important instruction in the higher tantras.

Rational mind, Tib. blo: The Kagyu and Nyingma traditions use this term pejoratively for the most part. In the Great Completion and Mahāmudrā teachings, this term specifically means the dualistic mind. It is the villain, so to speak, which needs to be removed from the equation in order to obtain enlightenment. This term is commonly translated simply as mind but that causes confusion with the many other words that are also translated simply as mind. It is not just another mind but is specifically the sort of mind that creates the situation of this and that (ratio in Latin) and hence upholds the duality of samsara. It is the very opposite of the essence of mind. Thus, this is a key term which should be noted and not just glossed over as "mind".

Rigpa, Tib. rig pa: This is the singularly most important term in the whole of Great Completion and Mahāmudrā. In particular, it is the key word of all words in the Great Completion system of the Thorough Cut. Rigpa literally means to know in the sense of "I see!" It is used at all levels of meaning from the coarsest everyday sense of knowing something to the deepest sense of knowing something as presented in the system of Thorough Cut. The system of Thorough Cut uses this term in a very special sense, though it still retains its basic meaning of "to know". To translate it as "awareness" which is common practice these days is a poor practice; there are many kinds of awareness but there is only one rigpa and besides, rigpa is substantially more than just awareness. Since this is such an important term and since it lacks an equivalent in English, I choose not to translate it. However, it will be helpful in reading the text to understanding the meaning as just given.

This is the term used to indicate enlightened mind as experienced by the practitioner on the path of these practices. The term itself specifically refers to the dynamic knowing quality of mind. It absolutely does not mean a simple registering, as implied by the word "awareness" which unfortunately is often used to translate this term. There is no word in English that exactly matches it, though the idea of "seeing" or "insight on the spot" is very close. Proof of this is found in the fact that the original Sanskrit term "vidyā" is actually the root of all words in English that start with "vid" and mean "to see", for example, "video", "vision", and so on. Chogyam Trungpa Rinpoche, who was particular skilled at getting Tibetan words into English, also stated that this term rigpa really did not have a good equivalent in English, though he thought that "insight" was the closest. My own conclusion after hearing extensive teaching on it is that rigpa is just best left untranslated. However, it will be helpful in reading the text to understanding the meaning as just given. Note that rigpa has both noun and verb forms. To get the verb form, I use "rigpa'ing".

Seat of rulership, Tib. btsan sa: The place at which one has gained total dominion over all else. It is the high place above all others which not only rules over all others but is unassailable by all others. In Great Completion literature, the term is especially used in relation to Thorough Cut practice where it is used as part of the metaphor of attaining to the governing position of re-connecting to one's innate, primordial reality. Extensive explanations of this can be found in the

Padma Karpo Translation Committee publication, *Empowerment and Ati Yoga* by Tony Duff.

Shamatha, Tib. gzhi gnas: The name of one of the two main practices of meditation used in the Buddhist system to gain insight into reality. This practice creates a foundation of one-pointedness of mind which can then be used to focus the insight of the other practice, vipaśhyanā. If the development of shamatha is taken through to completion, the result is a mind that sits stably on its object without any effort and a body which is filled with ease. Altogether, this result of the practice is called "the creation of workability of body and mind".

State, Tib. ngang: A key term in Mahāmudrā and Great Completion. Unfortunately it is often not translated and in so doing much meaning is lost. Alternatively, it is often translated as "within" which is incorrect. The term means a "state". A state is a certain, ongoing situation. In Buddhist meditation in general, there are various states that a practitioner has to enter and remain in as part of developing the meditation.

Stoppageless, Tib. 'gag pa med pa: A key term in Mahāmudrā and Great Completion. It is usually translated as "unceasing" but this is a different verb. It refers to the situation in which one thing is not being stopped by another thing. It means "not stopped", "without stoppage", "not blocked and prevented by something else" that is, stoppageless. The verb form associated with it is "not stopped" q.v. It is used in relation to the practice of luminosity. A stoppageless luminosity is the actual state of reality and what the practitioner has to aim for. At the beginning of the practice, a practitioner's experience of luminosity will usually not be stoppageless but with stoppages.

Superfactual, Skt. paramārtha,Tib. don dam: This term is paired with the term "fictional" q.v. Until now these two terms have been translated as "relative" and "absolute" but those translations are nothing like the original terms. These terms are extremely important in the Buddhist teaching so it is very important that their translations be corrected but, more than that, if the actual meaning of these terms is not presented, the teaching connected with them cannot be understood.

The Sanskrit term parāmartha literally means "a superior or holy kind of fact" and refers to the wisdom mind possessed by those who have developed themselves spiritually to the point of having transcended samsara. That wisdom is *superior* to an ordinary, un-developed person's consciousness and the *facts* that appear on its surface are superior compared to the facts that appear on the ordinary person's consciousness. Therefore, it is superfact or the holy fact, more literally. What this wisdom sees is true for the beings who have it, therefore what the wisdom sees is superfactual truth.

Superfactual truth, Skt. paramārthasatya, Tib. don dam bden pa: see under "Superfactual" for an explanation of this term.

Superfice, superficies, Tib. rnam pa: in discussions of mind, a distinction is made between the entity of mind which is a mere knower and the superficial things that appear on its surface and which are known by it. In other words, the superficies are the various things which pass over the surface of mind but which are not mind. Superficies are all the specifics that constitute appearance, for example, the colour white within a moment of visual consciousness, the sound heard within an ear consciousness, and so on.

Temporary experience, Tib. nyams: The practice of meditation brings with it various experiences that happen simply because of the meditation. These experiences are temporary experiences and not the final, unchanging experience, of realization.

Thorough Cut, Tib. khregs chod: the Dzogchen system has several levels to it. The innermost level has two main practices, the first called Thregcho which literally translates as Thorough Cut and the second called Thogal which translates as Direct Crossing. The meaning of Thorough Cut has been misunderstood. The meaning is clearly explained in the *Illuminator Tibetan-English Dictionary*:

> "Thorough Cut is a practice in which the solidification that sentient beings produce by having rational minds which grasp at a perceived object and perceiving subject is sliced through so as to get the underlying reality which has always been present in the essence of mind and which is called Alpha Purity in this system of teachings. For this reason, Thorough Cut is also known as Alpha Purity Thorough Cut."

The etymology of the word is explained in the Great Completion teachings either as ཁྲེགས་སུ་ཆོད་པ་ or ཁྲེགས་གི་ཆོད་པ་. In either case, the term ཆོད་པ་ is "a cut"; there are all sorts of different "cuts" and this is one of them. Then, in the case of ཁྲེགས་སུ་ཆོད་པ་, ཁྲེགས་སུ་ is an adverb modifying the verb "to cut" and has the meaning of making the cut fully, completely. It is explained with the example of slicing off a finger. A finger could be sliced with a sharp knife such that the cut was not quite complete and the cut off portion was left hanging. Alternatively, it could be sliced through in one, decisive movement such that the finger was completely and definitely severed. That kind of thorough cut is what is meant here. In the case of ཁྲེགས་གི་ཆོད་པ་, the term ཁྲེགས་གི་ is as an adverb that has the meaning of something that is doubtless, of something that is unquestionably so. A translation based on the first explanation would be "Thorough Cut" and on the second would be "Decisive Cut".

Other translations that have been put forward for this term are: "Cutting Resistance" and "Cutting Solidity". Of these, "Cutting Resistance" is usually a translation made on the basis of students expressing the "resistance to practice", etcetera. That is a complete misunderstanding of the term. The term means that that the practitioner of this system cuts *decisively* through rational mind, regardless of its degree of solidity, so as to arrive directly at the essence of mind.

Unaltered or uncontrived, Tib. ma bcos pa: The opposite of "altered" and "contrived". Something which has not been altered from its native state; something which has been left just as it is.

Vajra Vehicle, Skt. vajrayāna, Tib. rdo rje'i theg pa: See the glossary entry "Great Vehicle".

View, meditation, and conduct, Tib. lta sgom spyod: A formulation of the teachings that contains all of the meaning of the path.

Vipashyana, Tib. lhag mthong: The Sanskrit name for one of the two main practices of meditation needed in the Buddhist system for gaining insight into reality. The other one, shamatha, keeps the mind focussed while this one, vipaśhyanā, looks piercingly into the nature of things.

Wisdom, Skt. jñāna, Tib. ye shes: This is a fruition term that refers to the kind of mind, the kind of knower possessed by a buddha. The original Sanskrit term has many meanings but overall has the sense of just knowing. In Buddhism, it refers to the most basic type of knowing possible. Sentient beings could do this but their minds are obscured so, although they have the potential for knowing with the wisdom of a buddha, it does not happen. If they practise the path to buddhahood, at some point they will leave behind their obscuration and start knowing in this very simple and immediate way.

This sort of knowing is there at the core of every being's mind. Therefore, the Tibetans called it "the particular type of awareness which is always there". Because of their wording, it is often called "primordial wisdom" but that is too much. It simply means wisdom in the sense of the most fundamental knowing possible.

TIBETAN TEXT

༄༅། །རི་ཆོས་བསླབ་བྱ་ཉམས་ལེན་དམར་ཁྲིད་གོ་བདེར་བརྗོད་པ་
གྲུབ་པའི་བཅུད་ལེན་ཞེས་བྱ་བ་བཞུགས་སོ།།

༄༅། །བཀའ་དྲིན་མཚུངས་མེད་དཔལ་ལྡན་བླ་མ་དམ་པའི་ཞབས་ལ་གུས་པས་ཕྱག་འཚལ་ཞིང་སྐྱབས་སུ་མཆིའོ། །བདག་དང་བདག་གི་རྗེས་འཇུག་རྣམས་ཀྱི་རྒྱུད་ལ་ཟབ་ལམ་གྱི་རྟོགས་པ་ཕྱིན་ཅི་མ་ལོག་པ་མྱུར་དུ་སྐྱེས་ནས་ཚེ་འདི་ཉིད་ལ་གདོད་མའི་བཙན་ས་ཟིན་པར་བྱིན་གྱིས་བརླབ་ཏུ་གསོལ། །དེ་ལ་འདིར་སྔོན་གྱི་སྨོན་ལམ་ལས་འཕྲོ་རྣམ་པར་དག་པས་མཚམས་སྦྱར་ཏེ་ཟབ་གསང་རྫོགས་པ་ཆེན་པོའི་ཆོས་དང་དེ་སྟོན་པའི་བླ་མ་ལ་སྙིང་ནས་བློ་ཁེལ་ཞིང་ཉམས་ལེན་མཐར་སྐྱོལ་བར་འདོད་པའི་གང་ཟག་སྐལ་པ་ཅན་རྣམས་ཀྱི་འཇུག་སྒོར་རི་ཆོས་གནད་ཀྱི་བསླབ་བྱ་ཡང་གསང་རྫོགས་པ་ཆེན་པོའི་ཉམས་ལེན་དམར་ཁྲིད་ལག་བཅངས་སུ་གོ་བདེ་བར་འཆད་པ་ལ་སྤྱི་དོན་རྣམ་པ་གསུམ་གྱི་སྒོ་ནས་ཤེས་པར་བྱ་སྟེ། སྦྱོར་བ་ཆགས་ཞེན་གྱི་འཁྲི་བ་བཅད་ནས་བློ་ཆོས་ཕྱོགས་སུ་བཀོལ་ཏེ་རྒྱུད་སྦྱོང་ཚུལ། དངོས་གཞི་ལྟ་སྒོམ་སྤྱོད་པའི་སྒྲོ་འདོགས་བཅད་དེ་སྒྲུབ་པ་ཉམས་ལེན་གྱི་སྲང་དུ་གཞུག་ཚུལ། རྗེས་

ཐོབ་དམ་ཚིག་སྡོམ་པ་བསྲུང་ཞིང་ཚེ་འདིའི་ལས་གཞུག་ཆོས་ཀྱི་བསྡུ་རྒྱལ་
པོ། །དེ་ལས་དང་པོའི་དོན་ཅུང་ཟད་སྨྲ་བར་བྱའོ། །ཀྱེ་མ་འོ་སྐོལ་རྣམས་
ཀྱི་སེམས་ཞེས་བྱ་བ་རིག་རིག་ཏུར་ཏུར་པོ་འདི་ཀུན་ཏུ་བཟང་པོ་དང་དུས་མཉམ་
དུ་དང་པོ་ཉིད་ནས་བྱུང་བ་ཡིན་ཀྱང་། ཀུན་ཏུ་བཟང་པོས་རང་དུ་མཁྱེན་པས་
གྲོལ། རང་རེ་སེམས་ཅན་རྣམས་ཀྱིས་ངོ་མ་ཤེས་པས་འཁོར་བ་མཐའ་མེད་
དུ་འཁྱམས། རིགས་དྲུག་གི་ལུས་གྲངས་ལས་འདས་པ་ཞིག་བླངས།
བྱས་པ་ཐམས་ཅད་དོན་མེད་དུ་སོང་། ད་རེས་མི་ལུས་བརྒྱ་ལ་ལན་གཅིག་
ཐོབ་པའི་དུས་འདིར་འཁོར་བ་ངན་སོང་དུ་མི་སྐྱེ་བའི་ཐབས་ཤིག་མ་འགྲུབ་ན།
ཤི་ནས་གར་སྐྱེ་ངེས་པ་མེད་ཅིང་། འགྲོ་བ་རིགས་དྲུག་གང་དུ་སྐྱེས་ཀྱང་སྡུག་
བསྔལ་ཁོ་ན་ལས་མ་འདས། མི་ལུས་འདི་ཡང་ཐོབ་པས་མི་ཆོག་སྟེ་ནམ་འཆི་
ཆ་མེད་པས་ད་ལྟ་ཉིད་དུ་ཆོས་གཤའ་མ་ཞིག་བྱེད་དགོས། དེ་ཡང་འཆི་ཁར་
མི་འགྱོད་ཅིང་རང་གིས་རང་ལ་མི་ཁྲེལ་བ་རྗེ་བཙུན་མི་ལ་ལྟ་བུ་ཞིག་དགོས་ཏེ།
ང་མི་ལ་རས་པའི་ཆོས་ལུགས་ལ། །རང་གི་རང་ལ་མི་ཁྲེལ་བ། །ཞེས་
གསུངས། ཆོས་ལམ་དུ་འཇུག་པ་ལའང་ཆོས་གཟུགས་མཁན་སྤྱི་འགྲེས་ནི་
མི་ཆོག་སྟེ། ཚེ་འདིར་ལྟོས་ཀྱི་བྱ་བཞག་འདོད་ཡོན་གྱི་འཁྲི་བ་ཐམས་ཅད་
གཅོད་དགོས། དེ་མ་ཆོད་པར་བློ་སབ་སོབ་ཙམ་གྱིས་ཆོས་སྒོར་ལན་གཅིག་
ཞུགས་ཀྱང་། ཕ་ཡུལ་ནོར་རྫས་གཉེན་བཤེས་མཛའ་གྲོགས་སོགས་ལ་
ཆགས་ན། ཆགས་སེམས་དེས་རྒྱུ་དང་། ཆགས་ཡུལ་དེས་རྐྱེན་བྱས།
མཚམས་སྦྱོར་བར་ཆད་བདུད་ཀྱིས་བྱས་ཏེ། སླར་ཡང་འཇིག་རྟེན་ཐ་མལ་པ་
དང་འདྲེས་ནས་ལས་མཐའ་ལོག་པར་འགྱུར་བ་ཡིན། དེས་ན་གྲོང་ལྟོ་གོས་
གཏམ་གསུམ་ལ་བསྐྱུར་ནས་འཇིག་རྟེན་ཆོས་བརྒྱད་ལ་མ་ཆགས་པར་རྩེ་གཅིག་
ཏུ་ཆོས་ལ་བློ་སྒྲིལ་བར་བྱ་སྟེ། འཆི་བ་སྙིང་ཟུག་གི་དབེན་གནས་སུ། །

ཞེན་པ་གཏིང་ལོག་གི་སྒྲུབ་པ་པོ། །ཚེ་འདི་བློ་བཏང་གི་སྒྲུ་མཚམས་
བཅད། །སེམས་ཆོས་བརྒྱད་ཀྱི་མི་དང་མཇལ་འཕྲད་མེད། །ཅེས་རྒྱལ་བ་
ཡང་དགོན་པ་ལྷ་བུ་ཞིག་བྱེད་དགོས། དེ་མིན་ཆོས་བརྒྱད་དང་འདྲེས་པའི་
ཆོས་དེ་དུག་དང་འདྲེས་པའི་ཁ་ཟས་བཟའ་བ་དང་མཚུངས་པས་ཕུང་ཚབ་ཤིན་ཏུ་
ཆེ། ཆོས་བརྒྱད་དེའང་བསྡུ་ན་རེ་དོགས་གཉིས་སུ་འདུ་ལ་དེ་ཀ་དོན་ལ་
ཆགས་སྡང་གཉིས་པོ་ཡིན། ནང་གི་ཆགས་སྡང་ཕྱི་རོལ་རྒྱལ་བསེན་གཉིས་
སུ་བརྫུ་བས་བློ་ཆགས་སྡང་དང་མ་བྲལ་གྱི་རིང་ལ་རྒྱལ་བསེན་དང་མི་འབྲལ་
བས་བར་ཆད་ལ་ཟད་པ་མི་འོང་། དེས་ན་ཞི་ཕུག་ཏུ་ཆོས་བརྒྱད་ཚེ་འདིའི་
བློ་ཞེན་ཨེ་འདུག་རང་གིས་རང་ལ་ཡང་ཡང་བརྟགས་ནས་སྐྱོན་དེ་འདོར་བ་ལ་
ནན་ཏན་བྱ། ཆོས་བརྒྱད་ཞེ་ལ་བཅངས་ནས་ལྷར་སྣང་ཆོས་ལྷར་བཅོས་ཏེ་
གཡོ་སྒྱུས་བསྒྲུབས་པའི་ཡོ་བྱད་ཀྱང་ལོག་པའི་འཚོ་བ་ཡིན། ཕ་ཡུལ་སྤངས་
པས་ཆོས་ཕྱེད་གྲུབ་ཟེར་བ་ལྟར་ཕ་ཡུལ་རྒྱབ་ཏུ་བསྐྱུར་ནས་ཆ་མེད་ཀྱི་རྒྱལ་
ཁམས་འགྲིམས། གཉེན་བཤེས་དང་བཟང་འབྲལ་བྱས་ཏེ་ཆོས་ཀྱི་བཤོལ་
འདེབས་ལ་མི་ཉན། ནོར་རྫས་སྦྱིན་པར་བཏང་ནས་འཚོ་བ་བསོད་སྙོམས་
གང་བྱུང་ལ་བརྟེན། འདོད་ཡོན་མཐའ་དག་ལང་ཤོར་གྱི་བར་ཆད་དུ་ཤེས་པར་
བྱས་ལ་མི་འདོད་པའི་བློ་བསྐྱེད། ནོར་རྫས་ལྷ་བུ་ལའང་བག་ཙམ་གྱིས་ཆོག་
ཤེས་པར་མ་བྱས་ན་གཅིག་བྱུང་གཉིས་དགོས་ཀྱི་རིང་ལ་འདོད་ཡོན་བསླུ་བྲིད་ཀྱི་
བདུད་འཇུག་པ་ལ་ཆོགས་མེད། གཏམ་བཟང་ངན་གང་ལའང་བདེན་འཛིན་
རེ་དོགས་དགག་བསྒྲུབ་མི་བྱེད་པར་མི་ཤི་བའི་ཤུལ་གྱི་གཏམ་བཞིན་ཅི་ལབ་རྡུང་
རབ་ཏུ་ཆུག །མཚན་ལྡན་གྱི་བླ་མ་མ་གཏོགས་བསླབ་བྱ་དྲང་པོར་བཤད་
མཁན་ཕ་མ་ཡིན་ཀྱང་མི་ཡོང་བས་རང་ཆོད་རང་གིས་བཟུང་སྟེ་སྣ་ཐག་མི་ལ་མ་
ཤོར་བར་བྱ། རྣམ་པ་ཙམ་དུ་དང་རྒྱུད་རིང་བའི་སྒོ་ནས་ཀུན་གྱི་སྣ་མི་བསྲེག

པར་མཐུན་པས་འགྲོགས་ཤེས་པ་དང་། དོན་ལ་སྒྲུབ་པའི་གེགས་སུ་འགྲོ་ན་དྲག་ཞན་སུས་ཀྱང་བསླུ་ལ་མི་ནུས་པ་ལྟུགས་ཀྱི་ཕ་བོང་ལ་དར་ཡུག་བཏགས་པ་འདྲ་ཞིག་དགོས། ཀློང་གང་ནས་རྒྱབ་རྒྱབ་ལ་མགོ་གུག་གུག་བྱེད་པ་ལ་ཁའི་འཛགས་མ་འདྲ་བའི་མི་གཞི་སླ་མོ་དེས་མི་ཡོང་། སྒྲུབ་པ་ཉམས་ལེན་གང་ཡང་ཐོག་མར་བརྟམས་པ་ནས་མཐར་མ་ཕྱིན་གྱི་བར་དུ། སྟེང་ནས་ཐོག་བབས། འོག་ནས་མཚོ་བརྡོལ། ཡོགས་ནས་བྲག་རལ། འཆི་བ་སྒྲོག་ལ་བབས་ཀྱང་དམ་བཅའ་བཞག་རེ་སྙམ་དུ་ཞེ་མནའ་བོར་ལ་དེ་ག་བཞིན་དུ་མཐར་ཐོན་པའང་བྱེད། ཐུན་ཚོད། གཉིད་ཚོད། ཐ་ན་ཁམས་གསེང་ཟས་ཀྱི་ཚོད་སོགས་དང་པོ་རང་ནས་ལང་ཤོར་ལ་མ་བཏང་བར་རིམ་པས་སྲོལ་དུ་ཚུད་པར་བྱ། ལྷག་པར་སྤྲོས་བཅས་སྤྲོས་མེད་ཀྱི་དགེ་སྦྱོར་གང་ལའང་རེས་འཇོག་སྤྱངས་ལ་ས་སྟོང་ཐ་མལ་དུ་དར་གཅིག་ཀྱང་མ་ལུས་པའི་ཉམས་ལེན་བསྐུར་རྐང་སློམས་པར་བྱེད། མཚམས་ཀྱི་ཚེ་སྒྲུག་སྒོ་འདག་སྦྱར་རམ་མིན་ཀྱང་གཞན་དང་གདོང་མི་འཕྲད། ངག་མི་གཏོང་། བྱ་ར་མི་བྱེད། སེམས་ཅན་ཚུབ་ཀྱི་རྣམ་གཡེང་ཐམས་ཅད་ཅམ་གྱིས་བཞག་ནས། ཀློང་རོ་དོར། ལུས་གནད་ལེགས་པར་བཅའ། ཡིད་དྲན་རིག་གི་ཐོག་ཏུ་སྤྱང་ལ་བེ་ཕུར་བཏབ་པ་ལྟར་སྐད་ཅིག་ཀྱང་གཡོ་མེད་དུ་སྡོད་ཚུག་པ་ཞིག་དགོས་ཏེ། ཕྱི་ནང་གསང་བའི་མཚམས་དམ་པ་ལས་རྟགས་དང་ཡོན་ཏན་ཐམས་ཅད་མྱུར་དུ་འབྱུང་བ་ཡིན། ད་རེས་ཁག་ཆེ་བས་ཁོང་དང་འཕྲད། ངག་ཀྱང་བཏང་། དེ་ཕྱིན་ནས་དམ་པོ་བྱའོ་སྙམ་པས་དེ་ལྟར་ཐལ་ན་སྒྲུབ་པའི་གཡང་ཤོར་ནས་ཇེ་ལྷོད་ཇེ་ལྷོད་ལ་འགྲོ། དེས་ན་ཐོག་མ་ཉིད་ནས་སྡོད་ཐག་ཐད་ཀྱི་བཅད་ན་ཇེ་དམ་ཇེ་དམ་ལ་འགྲོ་ཞིང་སྒྲུབ་པ་བར་ཆད་ཀྱིས་མི་ཁྱེར་བ་ཡིན། གནས་ཀྱི་ཁྱད་པར་མཚན་ཉིད་བརྟག་ཐབས་མང་དུ་འབྱུང་ཡང་སྤྱིར་བཏང་གུ་རུ་རིན་པོ་ཆེ་

སོགས་གྲུབ་ཐོབ་གོང་མས་བྱིན་གྱིས་བརླབས་ཤིང་དམ་སེལ་ཅན་གྱིས་མ་བརྟེན་པ་དང་། ཤིན་ཏུ་དབེན་ཅིང་མཐུན་རྐྱེན་འཛོམ་སླ་བ་སོགས་རང་རང་གི་ཁམས་དང་བསྟུན་པ་འཐད། དུར་ཁྲོད་དང་གཉན་ཁྲོད་སོགས་གཞི་བདག་གདུག་པ་ཅན་གནས་པ་རྣམས་སུ་ཕྱི་ནང་གི་རྟེན་འབྲེལ་འགྲིགས་པ་མྱུར་བས་ནུས་པའི་རྩལ་གྱིས་ཆུན་ན་སྒོམ་ལ་བོགས་དེ་རང་ཆེ། མ་ཆུན་ན་བར་ཆད་ཀྱང་མང་། རྟོགས་པ་སློང་དུ་གྱུར་ཆོ་འགལ་རྐྱེན་ཐམས་ཅད་གྲོགས་སུ་འཆར་བ་ཡིན་པས་དེ་དུས་དུར་ཁྲོད་སོགས་སུ་གསང་སྤྱོད་བྱས་ན་ལྷག་པར་བཟང་། རྒྱུན་དུ་ཕྱི་ནང་གི་འདུ་འཛིའི་བྱ་བ་ཐམས་ཅད་བཏང་སྟེ་བྱར་མེད་དུ་གནས་པ་དོན་གྱི་བདེན་གནས་ཡིན། རྒྱུད་སྦྱོང་བ་དངོས་ལ། ཐུན་མོང་དུ་བློ་ལྡོག་རྣམ་པ་བཞི་དང་། ཐུན་མིན་སྐྱབས་སེམས་སྒྲིབ་སྦྱོང་ཚོགས་བསགས་རྣམས་ཁྲིད་ཡིག་བཞིན་རེ་རེ་ནས་ཉམས་ཀྱི་མྱོང་བ་ཐོན་ཐོན་གྱི་བར་འབད་ཅིང་། ཁྱད་པར་བླ་མའི་རྣལ་འབྱོར་ལ་ཉམས་ལེན་གྱི་སྲོག་ཏུ་བཟུང་ནས་བརྩོན་དགོས། དེ་མ་བྱས་ན་སྒོམ་སྐྱེ་བ་བུལ། ཅུང་ཟད་སྐྱེས་ཀྱང་གེགས་སྙང་། རྟོགས་པ་གཞའ་མ་རྒྱུད་ལ་སྐྱེར་མི་བཏུབ་པས་བཅོས་མིན་གྱི་མོས་གུས་དྲག་པོས་གསོལ་བ་བཏབ་པས། ཇི་ཞིག་ནས་ཐུགས་རྒྱུད་ཀྱི་དགོངས་པ་འཕོས་ཏེ་རྟོགས་པ་ཁྱད་པར་ཅན་ཅིག་གིས་བརྗོད་དུ་མི་ནུས་པ་རང་གི་ནང་ནས་སྐྱེ་བར་ངེས་ཏེ། བླ་མ་ཞང་རིན་པོ་ཆེ། གནས་པ་བསྐྱང་བ། ཉམས་མྱོང་བསྐྱང་བ། ཏིང་ངེ་འཛིན་བསྐྱང་བ་ལ་སོགས་པ་མང་བར་གདའ་སྟེ། མོས་གུས་ཀྱི་སྟོབས་ལས་བླ་མའི་བྱིན་རླབས་ཀྱི་རྟོགས་པ་ནང་ནས་སྐྱེ་བ་འདི་དཀོན་པར་གདའ། ཞེས་གསུངས། དེས་ན་རྫོགས་པ་ཆེན་པོའི་དོན་རྒྱུད་ལ་སྐྱེ་བ་སྔོན་འགྲོ་ལ་རག་ལས་པ་ཡིན་པས། རྗེ་འབྲི་གུང་པས། ཆོས་གཞན་དངོས་གཞི་ཟབ་པར་བྱེད་དེ། ངེད་འདིར་སྔོན་འགྲོ་ཟབ་པར་བྱེད།

ཅེས་གསུངས་པའི་དགོངས་པའང་དེ་ལྟར་ཡིན་པར་གདའ་འོ། །གཉིས་པ་དངོས་གཞི་ལྟ་སྒོམ་སྤྱོད་པའི་སྒྲོ་འདོགས་བཅད་དེ་སྒྲུབ་པ་ཉམས་ལེན་གྱི་སྲང་དུ་གཞུག་ཚུལ་ནི། ཐོག་མར་ཡིན་ལུགས་ཤེས་པའི་ལྟ་བ་ལ། འདི་ལྟར་རང་གི་སེམས་ཉིད་དོན་དམ་གཤིས་ཀྱི་གནས་ལུགས་དེ་ཐ་སྙད་བློས་བཟོ་བཅོས་ཀྱི་མཚན་མ་ཐམས་ཅད་དང་བྲལ་བར་རིག་ཐོག་ཏུ་གཏན་ལ་ཕབ་པས། རིག་པ་རང་བྱུང་གི་ཡེ་ཤེས་སུ་ཧྲེན་པར་ཤར་བ་ལ། ཚིག་གིས་བརྗོད་དུ་མེད། དཔེས་མཚོན་དུ་མེད། འཁོར་བ་ན་ངན་དུ་མ་སོང་། འདས་པ་ན་བཟང་དུ་མ་སོང་། སྐྱེ་མ་མྱོང་། འགགས་མ་མྱོང་། གྲོལ་མ་མྱོང་། འཁྲུལ་མ་མྱོང་། ཡོད་མ་མྱོང་། མེད་མ་མྱོང་། རྒྱ་གར་ཡང་མ་ཆད། ཕྱོགས་གང་དུའང་མ་ལྷུང་། མདོར་ན་ཡེ་ནས་དངོས་པོ་སྤྲོས་པའི་མཚན་མ་ཅན་དུ་ནམ་ཡང་གྲུབ་མ་མྱོང་བས་ངོ་བོ་ཀ་དག་སྟོང་ཉིད་བརྡལ་ཁྱབ་ཆེན་པོ། སྟོང་པའི་མདངས་མ་འགགས་པར་འཁོར་འདས་ཀྱི་ཆོས་ཁམས་རྒྱ་མཚོ་ཉི་མ་དང་ཉི་མའི་ཟེར་བཞིན་རང་སྣང་བས་ན་ཅང་མེད་བྱུང་ཆད་དུ་སྟོང་མ་མྱོང་བས་རང་བཞིན་ཡེ་ཤེས་ཡོན་ཏན་ལྷུན་གྲུབ་ཆེན་པོ། དེ་ལྟར་སྣང་སྟོང་ཟུང་དུ་འཇུག་པའི་རིག་པ་སྐུ་གསུམ་གྱི་བདག་ཉིད་གདོད་མ་གཤིས་ཀྱི་གནས་ལུགས་འདི་གའི་ཡིན་ལུགས་ཇི་ལྟ་བ་བཞིན་ངོ་ཤེས་པ་ལ་བློ་འདས་རྫོགས་པ་ཆེན་པོའི་ལྟ་བ་ཟེར། སློབ་དཔོན་ཆེན་པོས། བློ་འདས་ཆོས་སྐུ་དེ་བཞིན་ཉིད། །ཅེས་གསུངས། འོ་སྐོལ་རྣམས་ཀུན་ཏུ་བཟང་པོའི་དགོངས་པ་ལ་མངོན་སུམ་དུ་སྣར་འཛིན་བྱེད་པ་ལགས་ཏེ་ཨ་རེ་དགའ་ན། རྒྱལ་བས་ཆོས་ཀྱི་ཕུང་པོ་སྟོང་ཕྲག་བརྒྱད་ཅུ་རྩ་བཞི་ཕྱེ་བ་ཐམས་ཅད་ཀྱི་མཐར་ཐུག་རྫོགས་ཆེན་རྒྱུད་འབུམ་ཕྲག་དྲུག་ཅུ་རྩ་བཞིའི་སྙིང་པོ་དེ་འདི་རང་ཡིན། འདི་ལས་འགྲོ་ས་སྐར་མ་གང་མེད། འདིའི་ཐོག་ཏུ་ཆོས་ཐམས་ཅད་ཀྱི་སྣར་ཐག་གཅོད་དགོས་པ་ཡིན་

ནོ། །ད་དེ་ལྟ་བུའི་ལྟ་བ་ལ་ཐེ་ཚོམ་དང་སྒྲོ་འདོགས་ནང་ནས་ཆོད་པར་བྱས་ཏེ་
དེའི་རྒྱུན་སྐྱོང་བ་ལ་སྒོམ་པ་ཟེར་བ་ཡིན། གཞན་གཏད་སོ་དང་བཅས་པའི་
སྒོམ་པ་ཐམས་ཅད་བློས་བྱས་ཀྱི་རྟོག་སྒོམ་ཡིན་པས་ང་ཅག་དེ་འདྲ་མི་བྱེད།
སྔར་གྱི་ལྟ་བ་དེ་ཀ་རྩུགས་མ་ཤོར་བའི་ངང་ལ་སྒོ་ལྔའི་ཤེས་པ་ཐམས་ཅད་རང་
བབས་སུ་གློད་ནས་ལྷུག་པར་བཞག །འདིའོ་ཞེས་ཆེད་དུ་མི་བསྒོམ།
བསྒོམ་ན་བློ་ཡིན་པས་བསྒོམ་རྒྱུ་ཅི་ཡང་མེད། ཡེངས་སུ་སྐད་ཅིག་ཀྱང་མི་
འཇུག །རང་ཐོག་ཏུ་འཛོག་པ་དེ་ལས་ཡེངས་ན་འཁྲུལ་པ་དངོས་ཡིན་པས་མ་
ཡེངས་པར་བྱ། རྟོག་པ་ཅི་ཤར་ཡང་འཆར་དུ་བཅུག་ལ། དེའི་རྗེས་སུ་
ཡང་མི་འབྲང་། བཀག་ཀྱང་མི་བཀག །འོ་ན་ཇི་ལྟར་བྱ་ཞེ་ན། ཡུལ་
གྱི་སྣང་བ་ཅི་ཤར་ཅིར་སྣང་ཐམས་ཅད་བུ་ཆུང་ལྷ་ཁང་ལ་བལྟ་བ་ལྟར་སྣང་ཆ་ལ་
འཛིན་པ་མ་ཞུགས་པར་སོ་མར་བཞག་པས་ཆོས་ཐམས་ཅད་རང་ས་རང་ས་ན་
བཟོ་མ་ཉམས། མདོག་མ་འགྱུར། བཀྲག་མ་ཡལ་བར་སྣང་ཡང་དེ་ལ་
ཞེན་འཛིན་གྱི་རྟོག་པས་མ་བསླད་པས་སྣང་རིག་ཐམས་ཅད་གསལ་སྟོང་གི་ཡེ་
ཤེས་རྗེན་པར་འཆར་བ་ཡིན་ནོ། །ཡར་ཆོས་ཟབ་ཟབ་དང་རྒྱ་ཆེ་ཆེའི་མིང་
བཏགས་མང་པོ་ཞིག་གིས་བློ་དམན་ཀུན་མགོ་འཁོར་འདུག་པས། དོན་རྟོག་
རྟོག་ཕྱིལ་ཕྱིལ་མཇུབ་ཚུག་ཏུ་བསྟན་ན། རྟོག་པ་ཤར་མ་འགགས། ཕྱི་མ་མ་
ཤར་བའི་བར་དེར། ད་ལྟའི་ཤེས་པ་སོ་མ་བསྒྱུར་བཀོད་སྤྲུ་ཙམ་མ་སོང་བའི་
གསལ་རིག་རྗེན་ནེ་བ་ཞིག་མི་འདུག་གེ །འོ་དེ་ཀ་རིག་པ་རང་གི་བཞུགས་
ཚུལ་ཡིན། ཡང་རྟོག་པ་དེ་ཁོ་ནའི་ངང་དུ་མི་གནས་པར་རྣམ་རྟོག་ཅིག་ཐོལ་
གྱིས་འཆར་གྱི་མི་འདུག་གེ །དེ་རིག་པ་དེའི་རང་རྩལ་ཡིན། འོན་ཀྱང་དེ་
ལྟར་ཤར་མ་ཐག་ནས་ངོ་མ་ཤེས་པར་རྣམ་རྟོག་རང་རྒྱུད་པར་འབྱམས་ན་འཁྲུལ་
པ་ལུ་གུ་རྒྱུད་ཅེས་འཁོར་བའི་རྩ་བ་ཡིན། ཤར་མ་ཐག་ཏུ་ངོ་ཤེས་ཙམ་གྱིས་

རྗེས་མཐུད་མེད་པར་རང་གྲོལ་ཏུ་གློད་དེ་བཞག་ན་རྣམ་རྟོག་གང་ཤར་ཐམས་ཅད་རིག་པ་ཆོས་སྐུའི་ཀློང་དུ་ཞུམ་ཞུམ་གྲོལ་བ་འདི་ག་ཁྲིགས་ཆོད་ཀྱི་ལྟ་སྒོམ་གཅིག་ཏུ་དྲིལ་བའི་ཉམས་ལེན་དངོས་གཞི་ཡིན། དཔའ་རབ་རྡོ་རྗེས། གདོད་ནས་དག་པ་དབྱིངས་ཀྱི་ངང་ཉིད་ལས། །རིག་པ་ཐོལ་སྐྱེས་སྐད་ཅིག་དྲན་པ་དེ། །རྒྱ་མཚོའི་གཏིང་ནས་ནོར་བུ་རྙེད་པ་འདྲ། །སུས་ཀྱང་མ་བཅོས་མ་བྱས་ཆོས་ཀྱི་སྐུ། །ཞེས་གསུངས། འདི་ལ་རྡོ་རུས་གཏུགས་ཏེ་ཉིན་མཚན་ཡེངས་མེད་དུ་བསྒོམ་དགོས་པས་སྟོང་ཉིད་གོ་ཡུལ་དུ་མ་ལུས་པར་རིག་གྲོལ་རང་དུ་སྤྲུངས་ཤིག །ད་ནི་སྒོམ་པ་དེ་ལ་སྤྱོད་པས་བོགས་དབྱུང་ཞིང་ཉམས་ལེན་གྱི་ཕྲང་དུ་གཞུག་ཚུལ་ལ། གཙོ་བོར་ཕུར་ཚད་པ་ལྟར་བླ་མ་ལ་སངས་རྒྱས་དངོས་ཀྱི་འདུ་ཤེས་དང་སྐད་ཅིག་ཀྱང་མ་བྲལ་བས་སྙིང་ནས་གསོལ་བ་ཕུར་ཚུགས་སུ་འདེབས་པ་འདི་མོས་གུས་དཀར་པོ་ཆིག་ཐུབ་ཅེས་བྱ་བ་ཡིན་ཏེ་གེགས་སེལ་བོགས་འདོན་གང་ལས་ཀྱང་འདི་ལྷག །ལམ་ཐམས་ཅད་བཙན་ཆོད་དུ་འགྲོ་བ་ཡིན། སྒོམ་སྐྱོན་བྱིང་ཞིང་རྨུག་ན་རིག་པ་ཧུར་ཕྱུངས། འཕྲོ་ཞིང་རྒོད་ན་ཤེས་པ་ཁོང་གློད། རྒྱུན་དུ་སྒོམ་མཁན་གྱི་དྲན་རིག་ཏུར་ཏུར་པོ་དེས་ཆེད་དུ་གཟུར་བའི་འཛུར་དྲན་མ་ཡིན་པར་རང་ངོ་རང་ཤེས་མ་བརྗེད་ཙམ་པའི་དྲན་པས་ཟ་ཉལ་འགྲོ་འདུག་སྤྱོད་ལམ་མཉམ་རྗེས་གང་གི་སྐབས་སུའང་རྒྱུན་ཆགས་སུ་སྐྱོང་ཞིང་། བདེ་སྡུག་དང་ཉོན་མོངས་པའི་རྟོག་པ་སོགས་གང་ཤར་ཐམས་ཅད་ལ་རེ་དོགས་སྤོང་ལེན་གཉེན་པོས་གཞོམ་པ་སོགས་གཏན་ནས་མི་བྱེད་པར་ཁོ་རང་གི་ངོ་བོ་བདེ་སྡུག་གི་ཚོར་བ་ཇི་ལྟར་འདུག་པ་དེ་ཀ་རྗེན་ནེ། ཧྲིག་གེ །ཡེ་རེ་འཇོག་པ་སྟེ། ཐམས་ཅད་ལ་གནད་གཅིག་ལས་མེད་པས་བསམ་བློ་མང་པོས་མགོ་མ་འཁོར། སྣང་བྱའི་རྣམ་རྟོག་དང་ཉོན་མོངས་ཀྱི་སྟེང་དུ་གཉེན་པོའི་སྟོང་ཉིད་ལོགས་སུ་བསྒོམ་མི་དགོས་ཏེ། སྣང་བྱ་ཁོ་རང་

རིག་པས་ངོས་ཟིན་པ་དང་མཉམ་དུ་སྦྲུལ་གྱི་མདུད་པ་ཞིག་པ་ལྟར་རང་གྲོལ་དུ་འགྲོ་བ་ཡིན། འོད་གསལ་རྡོ་རྗེ་སྙིང་པོའི་སྒྲས་དོན་གྱི་མཐར་ཐུག་འདི་ལྟ་བུ་ཕལ་ཆེར་གྱིས་ཚིག་དུ་སྨྲ་ཤེས་ཀྱང་ཉམས་སུ་བླང་མ་ཤེས་པར་ནེ་ཙོའི་ཁ་ཏོན་བཞིན་དུ་སོང་ནས་གདའ། འོ་སྐོལ་རྣམས་བསོད་ནམས་ཤིན་ཏུ་ཆེ་བ་ཡིན་ནོ། །ད་དུང་ལེགས་པར་སེམས་དང་གོ་རྒྱུ་ཡོད་དེ། རང་ཅག་ཚེ་རབས་ཐོག་མ་མེད་པ་ནས་ད་ལྟའི་བར་དུ་འཁོར་བར་འཆིང་བྱེད་ཀྱི་དགྲ་མི་ཤ་བོ་དེ་གཟུང་འཛིན་གཉིས་པོ་འདི་ཡིན། ད་རེས་བླ་མའི་བཀའ་དྲིན་ལས་རང་གནས་ཀྱི་ཆོས་སྐུ་ངོ་འཕྲོད་པས་དེ་གཉིས་བྱ་སྤྲུ་མེ་ལ་བསྲེགས་པ་ལྟར་རྗེས་མེད་ཞུལ་མེད་དུ་གཏོང་བ་དེ་སྙིང་ཚིམས་པོ་མིན་ནམ། འདི་ལྟ་བུའི་མྱུར་ལམ་གདམས་ངག་ཟབ་མོ་ཐོབ་ནས་ཉམས་སུ་མ་བླངས་ན་ཡིད་བཞིན་གྱི་ནོར་བུ་རྡོའི་ཁ་ནང་དུ་བཙུག་པ་དང་འདྲ་སྟེ་རེ་ཕང་། སྙིང་མ་རུལ་བར་ཉམས་སུ་ལོངས་ཤིག །དེ་ཡང་ལས་དང་པོ་པའི་རིགས་ལ་རྣམ་རྟོག་ནག་པོ་ཁ་འབྲུམས་ཀྱིས་དྲན་པ་ཡེངས་སུ་བཅུག་ཡོང་བས་རྣམ་རྟོག་བརྟད་འགྲིལ་མང་ཙམ་འོག་འགྱུར་སོང་རྗེས་སྐབས་ཤིག་ན་དྲན་པ་རྗིག་གེ་སླེབས་ནས་ང་ཡེངས་འདུག་སྙམ་པའི་འགྱོད་པ་སྐྱེ་ཡང་། དེ་ཚེ་རྣམ་རྟོག་སྔ་མའི་གཞུག་གཅོད་དང་ཡེངས་པ་ལ་འགྱོད་པ་སོགས་གང་ཡང་མི་བྱ་བར་དྲན་པ་རྗིག་གེ་སླེབས་པ་དེ་ཀའི་ཐོག་ཏུ་རང་བབས་ཀྱི་རྒྱུན་བསྐྱང་བ་ཁོ་ནས་ཆོག །རྣམ་རྟོག་ལ་ཆོས་སྐུར་བལྟ་མི་སྤང་ཟེར་བ་གྲགས་ཆེ་ཡང་ལྷག་མཐོང་གི་རྩལ་མ་རྫོགས་རིང་ཆོས་སྐུ་ཡིན་ལོ་ཙམ་གྱི་ངང་ནས་ཞི་གནས་ཧད་པོར་བཞག་ན་ཅི་ཡིན་འདི་ཡིན་མེད་པའི་བཏང་སློམས་ལུང་མ་བསྟན་གྱི་སྐབས་སུ་ཚུད་དོགས་ཡོད་པས། དེས་ན་དང་པོའི་རིང་རྣམ་རྟོག་གང་ཤར་ལ་ཅེར་གྱིས་བལྟས་ནས་བརྟག་དཔྱད་བསམ་གཞིག་ཅེར་ཡང་མི་བྱ་བར་རྣམ་རྟོག་ངོ་ཤེས་མཁན་རང་གི་ཐོག་ཏུ་མི་ཤན་གྱིས་བྱིས་པའི་རྩེད་མོ་ལ་

བལྟ་བ་ལྟར་སྣང་མེད་རྩིས་མེད་གཡས་ཆུང་དུ་འཇོག །དེ་ལྟར་བཞག་པ་ན་རྟོག་མེད་རང་བབས་སུ་གནས་བདེ་བའི་ཆ་དེའང་བློ་བུར་ཐོལ་བྱུང་དུ་བཤིག་པས་སྐད་ཅིག་མ་དེར་སེམས་ལས་འདས་པའི་ཡེ་ཤེས་རྗེན་ལྷང་ངེར་འཆར་བ་ཡིན། ལམ་གྱི་སྐབས་སུ་བདེ་གསལ་མི་རྟོག་གསུམ་གང་རུང་གི་ཉམས་དང་མ་འདྲེས་པ་ཞིག་མི་འོང་ཡང་མཆོག་འཛིན་ཞེན་རློམ་རེ་དོགས་སྤུ་ཙམ་མེད་པར་བཞག་ན་གོལ་ས་དེས་ཆོད། རྒྱུན་དུ་གཡེང་བ་སྤྱང་སྟེ་དྲན་འདུན་རྩེ་གཅིག་པས་བསྒོམ་པ་གལ་ཆེ། རེས་འཇོག་དང་གོ་ཡུལ་ལ་འབྲུམས་ནས་ཞི་གནས་ཕྱོགས་མགོ་ཙམ་ལ་རང་མཐོང་སྐྱེས་ཏེ་ཉམས་མྱོང་ལ་གདར་ཤ་མ་ཆོད་པར་ཁ་ཁྲེར་དང་ཚིག་ཁྲེར་ལ་མཁས་པ་ཙམ་གྱིས་མི་ཕན་ཏེ། རྫོགས་ཆེན་ལས། གོ་བ་ལྷན་པ་འདྲ་སྟེ་གོག་ནས་འགྲོ། །ཞེས་དང་། ཉམས་ན་བུན་འདྲ་སྟེ་ཡལ་ནས་འགྲོ། །ཞེས་པ་ལྟར་ཡུལ་གྱི་རྐྱེན་བཟང་ངན་ཕྲན་བུ་རེས་ཀྱང་སྒོམ་ཆེན་པ་བསླུས་ནས་རྐྱེན་ཐོག་ཏུ་འཆོལ་ར་བ་མང་། སྒོམ་རྒྱུད་ལ་ཐེབས་ཀྱང་རྒྱུན་དུ་མ་བསྒོམ་ན་གདམས་ངག་ཟབ་མོ་དཔེ་ཆའི་ལོགས་ལ་ལུས་ཏེ་བློ་དྲིད་ཆོས་དྲིད་ཉམས་ལེན་དྲིད་ནས་སྒོམ་གཤའ་མ་སྐྱེ་དུས་མི་ཡོང་། སྒོམ་ཆེན་སྙིང་པ་ཉམས་ལེན་གསར་པའི་དང་ནས་མགོ་བོ་བ་ཚྭ་ཁ་ལེར་གྲུམ་ཉེན་ཡོད་པས་ཤིན་ཏུ་གཟབ་དགོས་སོ། །དེ་ལྟར་རྒྱུན་རིང་བར་གོམས་པས་ཇི་ཞིག་ན་མོས་གུས་སོགས་རྐྱེན་གང་ཡང་རུང་བ་ཞིག་གིས་ཉམས་མྱོང་དེ་རྟོགས་པ་ན་འཕར་ནས་རིག་པ་རྗེན་ལྷག་གེར་མཐོང་། མགོ་ཤུབ་ཕུད་པ་བཞིན་གུ་ཡངས་ཕྱེ་ལེར་འགྲོ། དེ་ནི་མ་མཐོང་བ་མཐོང་བའི་མཆོག་ཅེས་པ་ཡིན། འདི་ནས་རྣམ་རྟོག་སྒོམ་ལ་ཤར་ཏེ་གནས་འགྱུ་མཉམ་གྲོལ་དུ་འགྲོ་སྟེ། དེ་ཡང་དང་པོ་རྣམ་རྟོག་ངོ་ཤེས་པས་གྲོལ་བ་སྔར་འདྲིས་ཀྱི་མི་དང་འཕྲད་པ་ལྟ་བུ། བར་དུ་རྣམ་རྟོག་རང་གིས་རང་གྲོལ་བ་སྦྲུལ་གྱི་མདུད་པ་ཞིག་པ་ལྟ་བུ། ཐ་མ་རྣམ་

རྟོག་ཕན་མེད་གནོད་མེད་དུ་གྲོལ་བ་ཁང་སྟོང་གི་རྐུན་མ་ལྟ་བུ་ནམས་རིམ་པར་འབྱུང་ཞིང་། ཆོས་ཐམས་ཅད་རང་རིག་གཅིག་པུའི་ཆོ་འཕྲུལ་དུ་ཐག་ཆོད་པའི་ཡིད་ཆེས་དྲག་པོ་ཞིག་ནང་ནས་སྐྱེ། སྟོང་ཉིད་སྙིང་རྗེའི་ཐ་སྙོང་འཁྲུགས། འཁོར་འདས་གཉིས་ལ་འདམ་ཁ་ཟད། སངས་རྒྱས་དང་སེམས་ཅན་བཟང་ངན་མེད་པར་རྟོགས། ཇི་ལྟར་བྱས་ཀྱང་བློ་བདེ་ཆོས་ཉིད་ཀྱི་ངང་ཁོ་ན་ལས་གཡོ་མི་ཤེས་པས་ཉིན་མཚན་བར་མེད་དུ་འབྱམས་ཀླས་པས་ན། རྫོགས་ཆེན་ནས། རྟོགས་པ་ནམ་མཁའ་འདྲ་སྟེ་འགྱུར་བ་མེད། །ཅེས་པ་ལྟར་རྣལ་འབྱོར་པ་དེ་ལུས་ཐ་མལ་མི་རུ་སྣང་ཡང་སེམས་ཆོས་སྐུ་བྱ་རྩོལ་དང་བྲལ་བའི་དགོངས་པ་ལ་བཞུགས་པས་ས་ལམ་ཐམས་ཅད་བྱར་མེད་དུ་བགྲོད། མཐར་བློ་ཟད་ཆོས་ཟད་བུམ་པ་ཆག་པའི་ནམ་མཁའ་ལྟར་ལུས་རྡུལ་ཕྲན་དུ་དེངས། སེམས་ཆོས་ཉིད་དུ་དྭངས། གདོད་མའི་གཞི་དབྱིངས་ནང་གསལ་གཞོན་ནུ་བུམ་པ་སྐུར་འཁྱིལ་བ་ཞེས་བྱ་བ་ཞིག་ཡོང་རྒྱུ་རེད་པ། འོ་དེ་ནི་ལྟ་སྒོམ་སྤྱོད་པ་མཐར་ཕྱིན་པས་ཐོབ་ཏུ་མེད་པའི་འབྲས་བུ་མངོན་དུ་གྱུར་པ་ཞེས་བྱ་བ་ཡིན། ཉམས་དང་རྟོགས་པའི་སོ་མཚམས་དེ་དག་ཀྱང་གོ་རིམ་ཅན་དང་། གོ་རིམ་དང་བྲལ་བ་དང་། གཅིག་ཅར་ཉིད་དུ་སྐྱེ་བའང་འབྱུང་བ་ནི་གང་ཟག་གི་དབང་པོའི་ཁྱད་པར་གྱི་ཡིན་ཀྱང་འབྲས་བུའི་དུས་སུ་ནམ་དབྱེར་མ་མཆིས་སོ། །སྤྱི་དོན་གསུམ་པ་རྗེས་ཐོབ་དམ་ཚིག་སྡོམ་པ་བསྐྱང་ཞིང་ཚེ་འདིའི་ལས་གཞུག་ཆོས་ཀྱི་བསྒུ་རྩོལ་ནི། དེ་ལྟར་ལྟ་སྒོམ་སྤྱོད་པའི་ཉམས་ལེན་ལ་འབད་དུ་ཟིན་ཀྱང་རྗེས་ཐོབ་སྤྱོད་ལམ་ལ་ཐབས་མི་མཁས་པས་སྡོམ་པ་དང་དམ་ཚིག་ལས་ཉམས་པར་གྱུར་ན། གནས་སྐབས་སུ་ས་ལམ་གྱི་གེགས་དང་བར་ཆད་དུ་འགྱུར་ཞིང་མཐར་ཐུག་མནར་མེད་པའི་དམྱལ་བར་ལྟུང་ངེས་པའི་ཕྱིར་རྟག་ཏུ་དྲན་ཤེས་ཀྱི་བྱ་ར་དང་མ་བྲལ་བས་སྤང་བླང་ཕྱིན་ཅི་མ་ལོག་པ་ཞིག་ཅི་ནས་གལ་ཆེ་སྟེ།

སློབ་དཔོན་ཆེན་པོས། ལར་ལྟ་བ་ནམ་མཁའ་བས་ཀྱང་མཐོ། །ལས་རྒྱུ་འབྲས་བག་ཕྱེ་བས་ཀྱང་ཞིབ། །ཅེས་གསུངས། དེས་ན་ཧད་པོའི་བློ་སྟེངས་སྤྱངས་ལ་རྒྱུ་འབྲས་ལ་ཞིབ་པར་སྤྱོད། དམ་ཚིག་བཅས་སྡོམ་ཕྲ་ཞིང་ཕྲ་བ་ཡང་མ་ཉམས་པར་བསྲུང་ཞིང་ཉེས་ལྟུང་གི་དྲི་མས་མ་གོས་པར་བྱ། གསང་སྔགས་ཀྱི་དམ་ཚིག་ལ་རྣམ་གྲངས་མང་ཡང་བསྡུ་ན་རྩ་བའི་བླ་མའི་སྐུ་གསུང་ཐུགས་ཀྱི་དམ་ཚིག་ཏུ་འདུ། བླ་མ་ལ་མིའི་འདུ་ཤེས་སྐད་ཅིག་ཙམ་སྐྱེས་པས་ཀྱང་དངོས་གྲུབ་ལོ་བླར་འགྱུར་བར་གསུངས། དེ་ཅིའི་ཕྱིར་ཞེ་ན་ཡུལ་གཉན་པའི་གནད་ཀྱིས་ཏེ། གང་ཕྱིར་རྡོ་རྗེ་འཛིན་པ་ཡིས། །དངོས་གྲུབ་སློབ་དཔོན་རྗེས་འབྲང་གསུངས། །ཞེས་སོ། །དེས་ན་གང་སུ་ཡང་རུང་སྟེ་དང་པོ་བླ་མར་མ་བཟུང་བར་དུ་ནི་རང་ཉིད་ལ་རང་དབང་ཡོད་ལ། བླ་མར་བསྟེན་ནས་དབང་དང་གདམས་ངག་གི་འབྲེལ་ཕན་ཆད་དམ་ཚིག་མི་བསྲུང་བའི་དབང་མེད་དེ། དབང་བཞིའི་མཇུག་ཏུ་བླ་མ་དཀྱིལ་འཁོར་གྱི་གཙོ་བོའི་མདུན་དུ་བཏུད་དེ། དེང་ནས་བཅུམས་ཏེ་བདག་བྲན་དུ། །ཁྱེད་ལ་བདག་ནི་འབུལ་ལགས་ན། །ཁྱེད་ཀྱི་སློབ་མར་བཟུང་བ་དང་། །ཆ་ཤས་ཀྱང་ནི་སྤྱོད་དུ་གསོལ། །ཅེས་ཁས་བླངས་པ་འདིས་རང་ཉིད་རྗེ་ལྟར་ཆེ་ཞིང་བཙན་རུང་བླ་མ་ལ་གཉའ་ཤོར་ཟིན་པ་མ་ཡིན་ནམ། དེ་བཞིན་དུ། གཙོ་བོས་རྗེ་ལྟར་བཀའ་སྩལ་པ། །དེ་དག་ཐམས་ཅད་བདག་གིས་བགྱི། །ཞེས་དམ་བཅས་ནས་དེ་ཕན་ཆད་གང་གསུངས་མི་བསྒྲུབ་པའི་དབང་ཨེ་ཡོད། རང་གི་དམ་བཅས་པ་དེ་མ་བསྒྲུབ་ན་མིང་མ་སླན་ཀྱང་དམ་ཉམས་ཟེར་བ་ལས་འོས་མ་མཆིས། གཞན་ཡང་བླ་ཆེན་འཁོར་མང་བ། ནོར་ཕྱུག་པ། དབང་བཙན་པ། ཁ་ཐབས་བཟང་བ་རྣམས་ལ་དམ་ཚིག་ལྷག་པོར་བསྲུང་། དམན་ཆ་བཟུང་བའི་བླ་ཆུང་སྤྲང་པོའི་བརྟུལ་ཞུགས་ཅན་རྣམས་ལ་དམ་ཚིག

བསྒྱུར་མི་དགོས་པར་ཆཤད་པའང་མེད། གང་ལའང་ཁེ་ཉེན་གྱི་གནད་ཀ་གོ་བ་ཞིག་དགོས་པ་ལས་ཧ་ཅན་འཐོམ་ལངས་པ་བཞིན་བསྡད་པས་ཡོང་བ་མིན། དེ་ལྟར་དམ་ཚིག་བསྒྱུར་དགོས་པ་དེའང་བླ་མའི་དོན་དུ་འདུག་གམ་རང་གི་དོན་དུ་འདུག་སེམས་རྣལ་དུ་ཕབ་ལ་བསམ་མནོ་སྨིན་འཐག་འཐག་ཐོངས། བླ་མའི་དོན་དུ་འདུག་ན་དེ་རིང་རང་ལ་ཙམ་གྱིས་བཞག་པས་ཆོག་སྟེ་དེ་མིན་རང་མགོར་རང་གིས་ཐལ་བ་འདེབས་མི་རིགས། མཆེད་གྲོགས་ཀྱི་དམ་ཚིག་སྤྱིར་བཏང་དུ་སངས་རྒྱས་ཀྱི་བསྟན་པའི་སྒོར་ཞུགས་སོ་ཙོག་ལ་བཟང་པོར་བལྟ་ཞིང་དག་སྣང་སྦྱང་། གྲུབ་མཐའི་ཕྱོགས་ཞེན་དང་སྐུར་འདེབས་སོགས་སྤང་། བྱེ་བྲག་ཏུ་བླ་མ་གཅིག་དང་དཀྱིལ་འཁོར་གཅིག་གིས་བསྡུས་ཚད་རྡོ་རྗེའི་སྤུན་གྲོགས་ཡིན་པས་བརླས་བཅོས་འགྲན་སེམས་ཕྲག་དོག་གཡོ་སྒྱུ་སོགས་སྤངས་ཏེ་སྙིང་ནས་མཛའ་ཞིང་གཙུག་པར་བྱ། སེམས་ཅན་ཐམས་ཅད་བདག་གི་ཕ་མ་དྲིན་ཅན་ཤ་སྟག་ཏུ་འདུག་པ་ལ་ཨ་ཙ་མ། འདི་རྣམས་འཁོར་བ་ཐར་མེད་ཀྱི་སྡུག་བསྔལ་དྲག་པོས་གཟིར་བ་ལས་བདག་གིས་མ་བསྐྱབ་ན་སུ་ཡིས་སྐྱོབ་སྙམ་དུ་ཤས་མི་བཟོད་པའི་སྙིང་རྗེ་བསྒོམ་ལ་བློ་སྦྱོང་། སྒོ་གསུམ་ཅི་ནུས་ཀྱི་ཕན་པ་འབའ་ཞིག་སྒྲུབ་ཅིང་དགེ་བ་ཐམས་ཅད་གཞན་དོན་དུ་བསྔོ། རྒྱུན་དུ་བསམ་དགོས་རྒྱུ་ཆོས་དང་བླ་མ། སེམས་ཅན་གསུམ་ལས་མེད་པས་བསམ་པ་དང་ལག་ལེན་མ་འཆོལ། རྟགས་དང་མིང་གི་རྟོགས་ལྡན་དང་གྲྭ་པ་རྣམས་ལ་མ་འགྲན་པར་མ་མགལ་ཁ་རྟུ་ཆུག་ལ་རང་སེམས་ཆུན། འདི་ག་གལ་ཆེ་ཤོས་ཞིག་ཡིན་པས་ལྷག་བརྫུས་མ་འདེབས། གཞི་ནས་རང་དོན་ཚེ་ཕྱི་མ་ཁོ་ནར་བསམ་ན་ཟེར་བ་དེ་རང་གིས་བྱས་པ་ཞིག་དགོས་རྒྱུ་ལས། ཤེ་ཚོར་སྙིང་གཞན་གྱིས་བསྒྲུབས་པའི་དགེ་རྩ་ལ་རེ་དགོས་བྱུང་ན་ཕན་པ་དཀའ་བར་མཆིས་སོ། །དེས་ན་བློ་ཁ་ནང་དུ་བཀུག་སྟེ་སྦྱོར་བ་སྙིང་ནས་ངེས་པར་འབྱུང་བའི་

ཀློས་ཆེ་དང་སྒྲུབ་པ་མཉམ་པའི་དྲན་འདུན་བསྐྱོན་འགྲུས་དྲག་པོས་གཞི་བཟུང་། དངོས་གཞི་ལྷ་སྒོམ་ཟབ་མོའི་ཉམས་ལེན་ལ་གནད་དུ་བསྣུན་ཏེ། རྗེས་ཐོབ་དམ་ཚིག་བསླབ་སྡོམ་གྱི་ཚུལ་ལ་སྤྱང་བླང་འགལ་མེད་དུ་སྤྱོད་པའི་ལག་རྗེས་སུ་ཡོན་ཏན་རང་དབང་མེད་པར་ནང་ནས་སྐྱེ་སྟེ། རྫོགས་པ་ཆེན་པོ་ནི་སྡིག་ཅན་བཙན་ཐབས་སུ་འཚང་རྒྱ་བའི་ལམ་ཡིན་པའི་ཕྱིར་རོ། །དེ་ལ་ཟབ་དྲག་པའི་དབང་གིས་བར་ཆད་ཀྱང་ཡོད་པས་ཁེ་ཆེ་སར་ཉེན་ཆེ་བ་དང་འདྲ། དེའི་རྒྱུ་མཚན་རང་གི་སྔོན་བསགས་ཀྱི་ལས་ངན་ཐམས་ཅད་གདམས་ངག་གི་ནུས་པས་སློང་བའི་རྟགས་སུ་ཕྱི་རོལ་དུ་བདུད་ཀྱི་བར་ཆད་ཆོ་འཕྲུལ་འབྱུང་བའང་། སྒྲུབ་གནས་དེར་ལྷ་འདྲེས་གཟུགས་སྟོན་པ་དང་། མིང་ནས་འབོད་པ་དང་། བླ་མར་བརྫུས་ནས་ལུང་སྟོན་པ་དང་། འཇིགས་སྐྲག་གི་ཆོ་འཕྲུལ་སྣ་ཚོགས་ཉམས་སམ་རྨི་ལམ་དུ་འབྱུང་བ་དང་། དངོས་སུའང་གཞན་གྱིས་བརྡེག་བཙོག་ཧག་རྐུན་ན་ཚ་སོགས་མ་ངེས་པར་འབྱུང་བ་དང་། སེམས་ཐོག་ཏུ་དོན་མེད་པར་སྡུག་བསྔལ་དྲག་པོ་སྐྱོང་བ་དང་། སྐྱོ་ཞིང་དུ་སྙིང་འདོད་པ་དང་། ཉོན་མོངས་དྲག་པོ་སྐྱེ་བ་དང་། མོས་གུས་བྱང་སེམས་སྙིང་རྗེ་བྲི་བ་དང་། རྣམ་རྟོག་དཀྲར་ལངས་ཏེ་སྒྲོ་བྲབ་བྱེད་པ་དང་། ཕན་གཏམ་ལོག་པར་གོ་བ་དང་། རི་ཁྲོད་དུ་སྡོད་སྙིང་མི་འདོད་པར་དམ་བཅའ་གཏོང་སྙིང་འདོད་པ་དང་། བླ་མ་ལ་ལོག་ལྟ་སྐྱེ་བ་དང་། ཆོས་ལ་ཐེ་ཚོམ་ཟ་བ་སོགས་དང་། གཞན་ཡང་མ་ཉེས་ཁ་ཡོག་དང་། གྲགས་པ་ངན་པ་དང་། མཛའ་བོ་དགྲར་ལངས་པ་སོགས་ཕྱི་ནང་གི་རྐྱེན་མི་འདོད་པ་སྣ་ཚོགས་འབྱུང་བ་སྲིད། འོ་ན་ཚོ་ལྡོངས་ཚད་ཡིན་པས་ངོ་ཤེས་པར་གྱིས་ཤིག །ཁེ་ཉེན་གྱི་སོ་མཚམས་འདི་ན་ཡོད། བར་ཆད་དེའང་གནད་ཀྱིས་ཟིན་ན་དངོས་གྲུབ་ཏུ་འགྱུར། དབང་དུ་སོང་ན་གེགས་སུ་འགྱུར། འདི་ལ་དམ་ཚིག་དག་ཅིང་མོས་གུས་ལྷེམ་

བརྒྱུད་མེད་པའི་སྙིང་རུས་ཅན་གྱིས་བླ་མ་ལ་བློ་གཏད། སྙིང་བཅོལ། ཅི་མཛད་ཁྱེད་ཤེས་ཀྱིས་གསོལ་བ་ཕུར་ཚུགས་སུ་གདབ། རྐྱེན་ངན་དེ་འདོད་ཐོག་ཏུ་ཁྱེར་ཏེ་ཉམས་ལེན་ལ་དྲག་ཏུ་འབད་པས། ཇི་ཞིག་ན་རྐྱེན་ཁོའི་ཕོ་ཚུགས་རང་ཞིག་ལ་སོང་ནས་ཉམས་ལེན་ལ་བོགས་ཐོན། སྣང་བ་བན་མ་བྱུན་དུ་འགྲོ། བླ་མ་དང་གདམས་ངག་ལ་ཕྱུར་བས་ཀྱང་ཡིད་ཆེས་སྐྱེ། དབྱིན་ལྷོངས་བྱུང་ཡང་ཨཙུ་ཏྟི་སླམ་པའི་བློ་གཏིང་རྙེད་དེ་འོང་། འོ་དེ་ནི་ཚར་ཚད་ཡིན་ཏེ་རྐྱེན་ལམ་དུ་ལོངས་པས་ཚར་ལྷོངས་འཁྲིགས་པ་ཡིན། ཨ་ལ་ལ། ཕ་རྒན་ང་རང་ཆོ་ལ་དགོས་རྒྱུ་ནི་དེ་རང་རེད། ཁ་ཟ་འདོད་ལ་སྒྲིད་པ་འདར་ཁྲིལ་ཁྲིལ་མི་རོ་ལ་འཛབ་པ་ལྷུར་མ་བྱེད་པར་བློ་སྟོབས་བསྐྱེད་ཅིག །ཡང་གང་ཟག་བསགས་རྒྱབ་དམན་པ། དམ་སྟོམ་ལྷོད་པ། ལོག་ལྟ་ཆེ་བ། ཐེ་ཚོམ་མང་བ། ཁས་ལེན་མཐོ་ལ་ཉམས་ལེན་ཞན་པའི་སྙིང་ལ་རྟུག་དྲི་ཁ་བ་ཆོ་བླ་མའི་གདམས་ངག་དཔེ་ཁྲིའི་སྟེང་དུ་བཞུགས་སུ་གསོལ། རྐྱེན་ངན་དེ་ལ་ཤེ་སྤུར་འཐམ་ནས་རྗེས་སུ་འབྲངས་པས་བདུད་ཀྱིས་སླག་རྙེད་དེ་ངན་འགྲོའི་ལམ་དུ་ཁྲིད་པར་མཆི། ཨ་ཁ་ཁ། དེ་འདྲ་མི་འབྱུང་བར་བླ་མ་ལ་གསོལ་བ་ཐོབ། དེ་ཡང་ངན་རྐྱེན་ལམ་དུ་ལྷོངས་པ་ནི་ཙུང་ཟད་སླ་མོད། བཟང་རྐྱེན་ལམ་དུ་ལྷོངས་པ་འདི་ཤིན་ཏུ་དཀའ་བས་རྟོགས་པ་མཐོན་པོར་རློམ་པ་དག་ཀྱང་ཚེ་འདིའི་ཆེ་ཐབས་འབའ་ཞིག་ལྷུར་ལེན་པ་རྣམ་གཡེང་ལྷའི་བུའི་བདུད་ཀྱི་འབངས་སུ་བཀོལ་དོགས་ཡོད་པས་ཤིན་ཏུ་གཟབ་དགོས། ཡར་འགྲོ་མར་འགྲོའི་ས་མཚམས་སྒོམ་ཆེན་སྤྲང་ལ་འདེགས་ས་འདི་ན་ཡོད་པས་གོ་བར་གྱིས། ནང་གི་རྟོགས་པའི་ཡོན་ཏན་གྱི་རྩལ་ཁ་མ་རྫོགས་བར་དུ་ཉམས་མྱོང་གི་ལོ་རྒྱུས་གང་ཐོད་ཐོད་ལ་བཤད་དུ་མི་རུང་བས་ཁ་ཚུམ། གཞན་ཡང་ལོ་མཚམས་ཟླ་མཚམས་ཀྱི་སྡུག་ཡུས་མ་འདྲེན་པར་མི་ཆེ་ཁོ་ན་ལ་ཚད་བཙུགས་ནས་ཉམས་

ལེན་ལ་འབྱུང་། སྟོང་ཉིད་ཁ་ཁྱེར་གྱི་བློ་བྲིད་ནས་ཀུན་རྫོབ་རྒྱུ་འབྲས་ཀྱི་དགེ་སྦྱོར་ཁྱད་དུ་མ་གསོད། གྲོང་ཆོག་འདྲེ་འདུལ་སོགས་ལྟོ་ཕྱིར་གྲོང་ཡུལ་དུ་ཡུན་རིང་མ་སྡོད། དོན་མེད་ཀྱི་ལས། དགོས་མེད་ཀྱི་གཏམ། ཕན་མེད་ཀྱི་བསམ་མནོ་རྣམས་ཉུང་དུ་ཆུག །ཟོག་དང་གཡོ་སྒྱུ་སོགས་ཆོས་འགལ་གྱིས་མི་མགོ་མ་བསྐོར། འདོད་ཡོན་ལ་ཞེན་པས་གཞོག་སློང་དང་ཁ་གསགས་སོགས་ཀྱིས་ལོག་འཚོ་མ་སྒྲུབ། ལྟ་སྤྱོད་མི་མཐུན་པ་དང་སྡིག་པའི་གྲོགས་མ་བསྟེན། རང་སྐྱོན་རང་གིས་ཐོན། གཞན་གྱི་སྐྱོན་མཚང་མ་བརྗོད། ཐ་མ་ཁའི་རིགས་ཐམས་ཅད་དམ་སྲིའི་འཕྲུལ་དུ་གསུངས་པས་སླེང་ནས་སྤོངས། ཆང་འདི་དམ་རྫས་སུ་བརྟེན་བྱ་ཡིན་ཀྱང་ར་རོ་བ་ཙམ་དུ་བག་མེད་པར་མ་འཐུང་། དད་ཅན་གྱིས་བཀུར་སྟི་བསྒྲུབ་པ་དང་། དད་མེད་ཀྱིས་སྐུར་འདེབས་ངན་གཤོམ་སོགས་བཟང་འབྲེལ་ངན་འབྲེལ་གང་ཡང་ཁྱད་མེད་དུ་ལམ་དུ་ཁྱེར་ལ་སྨོན་ལམ་དག་པས་རྗེས་སུ་བཟུངས། དུས་ཀུན་ནང་དུ་རིག་པ་དཔའ་མ་ཞུམ་པར་གཟེངས་མཐོ་བའི་ངང་ནས་ཕྱིའི་སྤྱོད་ལམ་དམན་པའི་ས་བཟུང་། རྒྱལ་པོའི་གོས་གྱོན། བཟང་ངན་འབྲིང་གསུམ་ཐམས་ཅད་གོང་དུ་ཁུར། འཚོ་བ་ངན་ངོན་ལ་བརྟེན་ནས་རི་ཁྲོད་དུ་སྡོད་ཚུགས་ཟུངས། བློ་རྩེ་སྤྲང་པོ་ལ་གཏོད། གྲུབ་ཐོབ་གོང་མའི་རྣམ་ཐར་ལ་ཡང་དཔེ་གྱིས། སྨོན་ལམ་ལ་ཁག་མ་འགེལ་བར་ཆོས་མགོ་གཙང་སེང་ངེ་ཐོན་པ་རེ་གྱིས། འཕྲུལ་རྐྱེན་ལ་ཁག་མ་འགེལ་བར་རྐྱེན་གང་བྱུང་གི་ཐོག་ཏུ་ཚུགས་ཐུབ་པ་རེ་གྱིས། མདོར་ན་རང་སེམས་དབང་པོར་བཞག་ནས་མི་ཚེ་ཆོས་ལ་དྲིལ་ཏེ་འཆི་དུས་བློ་ལྷག་མེད་པར་རང་གིས་རང་ལ་མ་ཁྲེལ་བ་ཞིག་གྱིས། ཉམས་ལེན་ཐམས་ཅད་ཀྱི་གནད་ཀ་དེ་ན་ཡོད་དོ། །ནམ་ཞིག་འཆི་བའི་དུས་ལ་བབས་ཚེ་ནོར་རྫས་ཅི་ཡོད་སྒོང་དག་བྱས་ལ་ཁབ་གཅིག་ཙམ་ལའང་ཆགས་ཞེན་མེད་པར་བྱ། དེ་

ཡང་རབ་འཆི་ཁར་བྲོད་པ་སྐྱེ་བ། འབྲིང་འཆི་བ་ལ་མི་འཚེར་བ། ཐ་མ་ཤི་ཡང་མི་འགྱོད་པ་བྱ་བ་ཡིན་པས། རྟོགས་པའི་འོད་གསལ་ཉིན་མཚན་ཁོར་ཡུག་ཏུ་སོང་ན་བར་དོ་མེད་དེ་ལུས་རྒྱུ་ཞིག་པ་ཙམ་ཡིན། དེ་མིན་བར་དོར་གྲོལ་བའི་བློ་གདིང་འདུག་ན་གང་ལྟར་བྱས་ཀྱང་རུང་། དེ་ལྟར་མེད་ན་སྔར་ནས་འཕོ་བ་ཉམས་ལོག་ཏུ་ཚུད་པ་སྦྱངས་ཏེ་དུས་ལ་བབས་པའི་ཚེ་ལས་སྦྱར་བས་གང་དུ་མོས་པའི་ཞིང་ཁམས་སུ་འཕོས་ནས་དེར་ས་ལམ་གྱི་ལྷག་མ་བགྲོད་དེ་འཚང་རྒྱ་བར་འགྱུར་རོ། །དེས་ན་རང་རེའི་བརྒྱུད་པ་རིན་པོ་ཆེ་འདི་ལ་སྟོན་བྱུང་གི་ལོ་རྒྱུས་སྙིང་པ་ཙམ་མ་ཡིན་པར། དེང་སང་ཡང་ཁྲིགས་ཆོད་དང་ཐོད་རྒལ་གྱི་ལམ་ལས་རྟོགས་པ་མཐར་ཕྱིན་ཏེ་གདོས་བཅས་འཇའ་ལུས་འོད་ཀྱི་ཕུང་པོར་དེངས་བཞིན་པ་འདི་ག་ལྟར་ལ། ནོར་བུ་པོར་ནས་འཆིང་བུ་མི་འཚོལ་བར་གདམས་ཟབ་མཁའ་འགྲོའི་སྙིང་ཁྲག་འདི་ལྟ་བུ་དང་འཕྲད་པ་ནི་ཤིན་ཏུ་སྐལ་པ་བཟང་བ་ཡིན་པས་སེམས་ཀྱི་དཔང་བསྟོད་དེ་སྤྲོ་བ་བསྐྱེད་ལ་སྒོམས་ཤིག །དཔེ་འདིའང་རྗེས་འཇུག་རྣམས་ཀྱི་སྙིང་ནོར་དུ་བཟུངས་ཤིག་དང་ཕན་པ་ཆེན་པོ་འབྱུང་བར་སྲིད་དོ། །ཞེས་པའང་འོག་མིན་པདྨ་འོད་གླིང་གི་སྒོམ་གྲྭ་བ་རྣམས་ཀྱི་རི་ཆོས་ཉམས་ལེན་དུ་དམིགས་པའི་རྒྱུ་བྱས། མི་ཕྱེད་པའི་དད་གུས་ཀྱི་ནོར་ལྡན་སྒྲུབ་བརྩོན་རིག་བཟང་རྡོ་རྗེས་བསྐུལ་བའི་རྐྱེན་བྱས་ཏེ། འཇིགས་བྲལ་ཡེ་ཤེས་རྡོ་རྗེས་སྙིང་གཏམ་བསླབ་བྱ་དམར་ཁྲིད་ཀྱི་ཚུལ་དུ་བརྗོད་པ་སྐལ་ལྡན་རྣམས་ཀྱི་རྒྱུད་ལ་རྟོགས་པའི་ཡེ་ཤེས་བཙན་ཐབས་སུ་སྐྱེ་བའི་རྒྱུར་གྱུར་ཅིག། ||

INDEX